Child Care Options

A Workplace Initiative for the 21st Century

Margery Leveen Sher and Madeline Fried

Foreword by Elinor Guggenheimer,
Founding President, Child Care Action Campaign

Oryx Press
1994

The rare Arabian Oryx is believed to have inspired the myth of the unicorn. This desert antelope became virtually extinct in the early 1960s. At that time several groups of international conservationists arranged to have 9 animals sent to the Phoenix Zoo to be the nucleus of a captive breeding herd. Today the Oryx population is over 800 and nearly 400 have been returned to reserves in the Middle East.

© 1994 by Fried & Sher, Inc.
Published by The Oryx Press
4041 North Central at Indian School Road
Phoenix, Arizona 85012-3397

Published simultaneously in Canada
Printed and Bound in the United States of America

∞ The paper used in this publication meets the minimum requirements of American National Standard for Information Science—Permanence of Paper for Printed Library Materials, ANSI Z39.48, 1984.

Library of Congress Cataloging-in-Publication Data

Sher, Margery Leveen.
   Child care options : a workplace initiative for the 21st century / by Margery Leveen Sher and Madeline Fried.
      p.   cm.
   Includes bibliographical references and index.
   ISBN 0-89774-858-1 (acid-free paper)
   1. Employer-supported day care—United States. 2. Work and family—United States. I. Fried, Madeline. II. Title.
HF5549.5.D39S54   1994
331.25—dc20   94-22547
                                                                        CIP

For Jeremy and Adam, and for Laura,
for whom child care was an exciting adventure.

Contents

Foreword

At various times during this century, in various studies, it has been predicted that the number of women in the labor force would decrease. In fact the opposite has been true; there has been an overwhelming increase in the number of women in the labor force. Today our national economy, the prosperity of individual companies, and the financial security of individual families often depend on women. Most company executives and partners in professional firms have come to realize that family needs have an impact on productivity. Well-informed people in our society have come to realize that most of our social problems, from the cost of welfare to failures in the school systems to the enormous cost of dealing with dysfunction and crime, can be traced to neglect and abuse of children. We see, increasingly, that these problems begin with society's failures in dealing with the needs of infants and children and with pressures on families.

What is not needed is another study highlighting the damage that has resulted from the neglect of young children. All of us should be concerned by the increasing numbers of single-parent families and by the need for second incomes that has driven mothers with children less than a year old into the labor market. We have failed to offer the care for children that is available to families in other parts of the world. Certainly the difficulty President Clinton faced in finding a U.S. attorney general indicated clearly the problems families face in finding quality child care. Business leaders have lacked clear guidelines on providing support for their workers, for whom they not only bear some responsibility but whose productivity is essential to their own success.

This very important book examines the business community's responsibility to its employees and ways in which this responsibility can be met.

Child Care Options is a long overdue resource that should be on the desk of every employer in our country, whether his or her business is a Fortune 500 company or a small business with less than 50 employees. In good conscience, no one in today's world should assume responsibility for providing services or products without assuming responsibility for his or her employees, and for their families.

Assuming responsibility involves understanding child care problems and how to solve them. Anyone who has struggled to put together a product that "needs assembly" will be grateful for the clear and well-documented instructions on providing child care in this book. With information on why business should be involved in child care, various options, potential pitfalls, and legal and liability issues, Fried and Sher have included in one volume everything a company executive needs to know about planning and managing a child care facility.

Many of us, and I among them, have struggled for years to bring this country into a competitive position with other industrial countries. I care about what has been happening to families and children in America, but I care, too, about our competitive position in a multinational economy. When a major part of the labor force is handicapped by our failure to give the support that every other industrial country offers to families with young children, I believe there is cause for the business community to be concerned.

Quality child care is good for working families, good for America's future, and good for business. The authors tell us why and explain how to remedy present neglect. The book is carefully researched, and the appendixes contain valuable additional information. *Child Care Options* is practical and informative and deserves to become the bible for those who are thinking about supporting our work force by supporting child care. In fact this might well be the ideal gift to give a harried businessperson who is wondering why productivity seems to go down at certain times of the day and at certain periods in the year.

Read and learn!

Elinor Guggenheimer
Founding President, Child Care Action Campaign

Preface

The Earth Shifts:
Babies 1, Football Game 0

Child care. Elder care. Family-friendly. Work-family. Work-life. Diversity. Since the late 1980s, new concepts for corporate executives to consider have sprung up at a rapidly increasing rate. The fact is the earth has definitely shifted. The quintessential work-family conflict was reported in the fall of 1993. Houston Oilers offensive lineman David Williams missed a game in order to stay with his wife and newborn son. Yes, a football player, an icon of masculinity, chose to cuddle his wife and baby and skip one game. And yes, the brouhaha was enormous. His line coach was irate. He remembered 20 or 30 years back and said, "My wife told me she was having a baby and I said, 'Honey, I've got to go play a football game.' "[1] On the other side, a "chorus of critics"[2] stood up for Williams and urged the Oilers not to fine or suspend him. They didn't.

And consider this: the no-nonsense *Wall Street Journal* regularly features a work and family column. Back in 1991, Sue Shellenbarger presented her ideas for the column, and the column has appeared regularly since July 1991 to the *Journal*'s 6 million readers. The response to the column has been tremendous. Katharine Hazzard, coordinator of Work/Family Programs at John Hancock comments, "The column has made work and family a business issue by virtue of its appearing on a regular basis. It has really awakened executive suites to the fact that these are real issues."[3] The column not only taps into businesspeople's need for current, cutting-edge work and family information but also elicits a wide-ranging emotional response from people who are actually experiencing the types of situations discussed. Shellenbarger notes the "emotional depth of the response" to her column from managers, rank-and-file workers, and even from family members of workers with work-family stresses.[4]

It is now almost O.K. to admit on Monday through Friday that one has a family. In recent years businesses began to acknowledge this by taking a look at the child care needs of their employees. But let's look back a bit at child care history. During wartime (even the Civil War), child care programs were organized so that women could work and keep the factories open. When the men returned from war, the child care programs closed. This cycle began to change in the late 1960s. At that time, corporate-supported child care had a slight surge because of women's increasing participation in the labor force and a climate of social responsibility. Many of these early child care centers closed, however, more often due to the failure of the companies than to the centers. During the 1970s, employer-supported child care was referred to as a "miniature curiosity" in one publication on women and work.[5] Failures were most often attributed to employers' attempts to provide top-grade services with little or no financial burden to parents. A good example is the Intermedics center, which opened in 1979 and closed in 1985. It was an excellent center, serving children of employees of the Texas pacemaker manufacturer and offering far more services than were usual, but parents were only charged $15 per week. When the company hit a cost-cutting climate, the center could no longer be justified.[6]

After this round of interest, employer-supported child care did not get off the ground again until the second half of the 1980s. Employers now are much more interested in the bottom line. The amount of an ongoing subsidy, if any, is generally planned for and budgeted for, and many centers are operating well on firm financial footing. The number of employers with some sort of child care program has increased from 600 employers in 1982 to an estimated 5,600 in 1990. This number represents 13 percent of the 44,000 employers with more than 100 employees. In 1993, approximately 2,200 employers sponsored child care centers, and the number continues to grow steadily. Approximately 1,000 centers are affiliated with hospitals, 900 with government agencies (including the Department of Defense), and 300 with corporations.[7]

By 1990, child care was being considered in the context of integrating work and family. Employers were beginning to recognize that workers needed assistance in dealing with dependent care issues—child care, as well as caring for elderly parents—in order to be more productive and loyal employees. The term "sandwich generation" was coined, representing those workers, usually in their thirties and forties, who have both elder and child care responsibilities.

A few years later, the notion of work and family in balance began to be replaced by work-life programs. Some employers began to consider the whole concept of life outside the workplace, including the concerns of those employees who have no need for child care or elder care services. It would seem, though, that to equate someone who wants a more flexible work schedule in order to improve a tennis game with someone who must care for a dying parent is an unnecessary permutation of a concept. Work-life became a work–life cycle concept in some companies, acknowledging that employees have different home-life needs that may affect work at different stages in their lives. Some companies also began to realize that work and family programs can be linked with diversity in the workplace. These companies attempted to organize work-family issues, minority issues, women's issues, and wellness issues under the rubric of diversity.

This transformation of thinking, however, has taken place only in a tiny percentage of companies and in the newspapers. The huge majority of companies in the country have not changed their policies to meet the needs of working parents. The issues have been in the limelight only since the mid-1980s, and several of these years have seen businesses struggling with the effects of recession. So, although the same 10 or so companies with child care centers are frequently cited—such as Campbell Soup, Fel-Pro, Stride Rite, Merck, John Hancock, Johnson & Johnson, Johnson Wax, Corning, Hoffman La Roche, Zale Corporation—and, again, 10 or so companies with strong work-family programs are frequently noted—including Xerox, American Express, IBM, US West, Aetna Life, Dupont, NationsBank, Johnson & Johnson, and Corning[8]—most American businesses are still in the thinking stages. The demographics of the work force are changing, but what, if anything, do companies need to do?

Directed toward decision makers in both commercial and nonprofit organizations and employees who need better child care, this book discusses numerous child care alternatives in depth as well as some general work-family options, places child care in the work-family arena, and suggests a model for considering work-family within the context of diversity management. We have attempted to discuss child care as it is placed in the human resource agenda, but we have chosen to focus on an intensive study of child care options. Several chapters are devoted to the legal, financial, and operational details of various types of child care programs. Even though child care is but one segment of a comprehensive work-family program, we concentrate on child care because its impact is so far-reaching. Employees' need for child care will only grow as demographic trends continue. More and more businesses are becoming involved in helping their employees locate and pay for child care and in increasing the supply of child care by developing their own child care centers, helping existing programs expand, and supporting recruitment efforts for family child care providers. The majority of the child care programs in this country, however, are poor quality, so businesses must support and strengthen high-quality programs, not just any programs. This book seeks to provide people with the information needed to select the most appropriate child care alternative and to develop programs that are exemplary and will foster the positive development of children.

Child Care Options is based on the authors' 25 years of experience in the child care field, including the nine years of work-family projects undertaken by Fried & Sher, Inc. All Fried & Sher staff have provided most valuable input. The first and last chapters place child care into the context of current and future demographics and trends. Chapters 2 and 3 discuss a multitude of choices and how to decide which option is right for your business. Chapters 4 through 9 divulge the legal, financial, design, and management details of direct-service child care (such as full child care centers, emergency back-up care, consortia, and school-age programs). Chapter 10 is addressed specifically to small businesses. Nine appendixes provide supplemental information, including listings of corporate-supported child care, insurance carriers, licensing information, architectural and playground resources, and important organizations. Appendix A is a synopsis of the points made in each chapter, which may be helpful in making formal presentations.

One of our goals in writing the book was to present in a clear, concise format useful information that business and nonprofit organization managers need to make an appropriate decision about instituting a child care service. An adjunct goal was to produce a book that was fun to read. We hope we have succeeded.

Child care is not a passing trend. It is an integral part of a work-family agenda in a diverse work force, and it is an essential issue for corporations to consider in order to be competitive in the twenty-first century. Child care is a productivity issue for companies today as well as an issue affecting the quality of the workers of the next generation.

NOTES

1. Leonard Shapiro, "Oilers' Williams Experiences Labor Pains," *Washington Post,* October 20, 1993, C4.

2. Sue Shellenbarger, "Work & Family," *Wall Street Journal,* October 25, 1993, B1.

3. Personal conversation with Katharine Hazzard, April 29, 1994.

4. Telephone interview with Sue Shellenbarger, April 21, 1994.

5. E. Galinsky, D. E. Friedman, and C. L. A. Hernandez, *The Corporate Reference Guide to Work-Family Programs* (New York: Families and Work Institute, 1991), 111.

6. Dana E. Friedman, "The Intermedics Story," *Business Link* (April 1986), 3.

7. Telephone conversation with Dana Friedman, October 1993.

8. Sue Shellenbarger, "Work & Family: So Much Talk, So Little Action," *Wall Street Journal,* June 21, 1993, R4.

Acknowledgments

This book is truly a collaboration of the knowledge and insights of the entire Fried & Sher team. Kathy Steiner, Fried & Sher's resource coordinator, provided input into each chapter. Her skills in maintaining up-to-date information on the broad range of work-family issues have been vital to the development of this book. Kathy's thought processes and writing skills are an integral part of chapter 1. Susan Jones's research and her ideas for additions, charts, and summaries are evident in each chapter. Pam Wayland painstakingly worked through the word processing details and contributed a great deal to the final manuscript. The contributions of our senior consulting staff, Joanne Pfeil, Lynn Wilson, and Annette Dubrouillet, were indispensable. Joan Denney, our financial manager, provided insight and examples for chapter 6. Our center directors, Leslie Switzer and Carolyn Elverenli, were the models for excellent management, described in chapters 8 and 9.

Our clients and corporate friends have been most generous with their time and their quotes, and we thank them all.

Special thanks to the Oryx Press—Susan Slesinger and Natalie Lang for their vision for the book and concrete ideas, and Kristan Martina for her impressive editing skills and excellent suggestions.

To Florence Janovic, a multitude of thanks for her encouragement and guidance.

For their love and support, much gratitude to Gerson, Jeremy, and Adam Sher.

Chapter One

■ ■ ■ ■ ■

Child Care!
What Does That Have to Do
with Our Business?

George Oliver strode briskly into the board room. His first glance took in the whole scene and he smiled briefly at his team. He enjoyed these semiannual strategic planning meetings with his senior executives. This was the time and place to push decisions that would move GO Systems forward.

Sunlight streamed in through the 37th floor windows, and the room looked serene in the light, muted by Belgian lace draperies. The executives stopped their conversations and waited for George to begin.

"Good morning. As usual, our agenda is to assess where we are in each of your bailiwicks and to make some decisions that will move us forward. Let's start with you, Elinor, with the finances."

Over the next hour, Elinor Mackingham dissected the company's finances for the group. Profits were inching upward but were stymied by turnover and the accompanying costs of recruitment and new employee training. Elinor displayed charts that showed spiraling costs in these areas for the last two years.

Duncan Greenway, vice president for marketing, was next. Duncan wanted a new direction for marketing. He noted that GO Systems' marketing was rather traditional, while he had learned that two major competitors, one in Dallas and one in Chicago, were using a new tack, which had generated much free publicity for them. They were presenting themselves as caring corporate citizens and were donating employee time and money to community projects. The Dallas company was supporting housing projects for the needy, and the Chicago company sent its employee volunteers into the public schools as tutors. Duncan had calculated the value of the free publicity, and it was impressive. As Duncan sat down, he wondered if he could get the company involved in his pet project, the Eastside Soup Kitchen.

David Stone, vice president for quality, described the internal focus groups he had held during the last two months. He had initiated the focus group process after hearing comments about family problems and employees who were not concentrating on their work. The focus groups corroborated the rumors. Younger employees were plagued by child care problems. They could not find quality reliable care that they could afford. Other employees were sympathetic but were upset that their own work was being affected by their coworkers' problems. The situation was definitely having an impact on work teams.

The human resources vice president, Bob Roman, listened to David's report with a sense of relief. He too was prepared to bring up the issue of child care, but he was nervous. Child care was a world away from GO Systems' business. He worried about equity of benefits and the costs of a new program. When his assistants first brought up the idea, Bob was highly skeptical. After studying the latest demographic data on the employees, however, he thought the idea bore some consideration. Still, he had not relished the idea of raising the issue at this meeting. David's report certainly laid the groundwork for him.

The other vice presidents followed with well-substantiated, concise analyses of their areas. By the end of the meeting, research into the child care issue had been written into the six-month plan. The original working paper was to be drawn up by the human resources department for the next semiannual meeting.

George left the meeting feeling satisfied. Several new plans were to be put into effect immediately. Others were in beginning stages to be considered over the next year. The child care idea was certainly farfetched, but at least they hadn't spent too much time on it.

It was nine that evening when the phone rang. George had just settled down in his old leather chaise in the library. Marilyn was comfortable reading in the big chintz easy chair, with her precious 40-year-old afghan draped over her legs. The housekeeper knocked softly on the library door.

"Mr. Oliver, your daughter's on the phone."

George smiled. Alison was his pride. A brilliant attorney. If only she didn't live 1,000 miles away. George glanced at Marilyn and picked up the phone.

"Hi, darling!" he boomed.

"Daddy! I have exciting news! You're going to be a grandfather!"

In this pat tale lurk many truths. Elinor Mackingham's concerns with recruitment and new employee training costs are reflected in many companies, and child care programs and other work-family programs have been shown to reduce these costs. In May 1993, the University of Chicago released its study of work-family programs at Fel-Pro. The study indicated that employees who most utilize work-family benefits have the highest job performance evaluations and are the least likely to think of leaving the company.[1] A second study, conducted by Families and Work Institute, also attracted media attention in May 1993. This study of Johnson & Johnson employees found that those who perceive their supervisors and the company culture as more supportive of their need to balance work and family are more loyal, more likely to recommend the company as a place to work, and more satisfied with their jobs.[2] Admiral J. William Kime, commandant of the Coast Guard, has initiated a wide-ranging work-family program. He notes that the Coast Guard now has a higher reenlistment rate than ever before, and, as a result, training costs for new recruits are significantly lower.[3]

While reduced turnover and improved recruitment have been shown to be the most significant benefits of employer-supported child care, some companies have been especially gratified by the enormous benefits reaped in free publicity, as our fictitious Duncan Greenway noted. The *Wall Street Journal,* in a 1993 summary of the research on corporate child care centers, stated that it is clear that centers yield favorable publicity.[4] Union Bank, for example, cited 27 newspaper and magazine articles, two evening television news spots, and a radio program for a total estimated worth of $40,000 in free advertising. This kind of public relations has been valuable both in attracting customers and recruiting employees. Attention to the issue in business journals increases annually. In the fall of 1993, family programs were featured in *Fortune, Business Week, Newsweek, HR News,* the *New York Times,* the *Washington Post,* and the *Wall Street Journal.* *Working Mother* compiles a list each year of "The Best Companies for Working Mothers in America" (see Table 1.1). According to the *Wall Street Journal*, entries are up in 1993. "As the biggest companies vie for a family-friendly image, entries . . . have surged to 300, 30 percent more than in 1992, swamping the judges in glossy brochures."[5]

As David Stone's focus groups showed, one worker's problems often affect others on the team, and employees without young children are usually quite supportive of child care programs for this reason. While some companies are reluctant to address child care issues because they fear equity problems, others have found this not to be the case. In fact, there have been reports of CEOs receiving letters from nonparents thanking them for caring about families.[6] As the work-family movement evolves, equity issues are being addressed in creative ways and are becoming less of a problem. Child care programs are being viewed as one important spoke in the life-cycle approach to benefits, which may include a variety of benefits ranging from adoption subsidies to assistance with college tuitions to a resource and referral service for elder care. Concerns about equity in benefits and costs, however, are common to executives considering child care—as they were to Bob Roman.

In the weeks ahead, as George Oliver's daughter shares with him her anxieties and excitement about the pregnancy, he finds himself thinking

Table 1.1
1993 *Working Mother's* 10 Best Companies

| Companies | Family-Friendly Options | | | |
	Flexible Work Options	Child Care	Elder Care	Benefits
AT&T 32 Avenue of the Americas New York, NY 10013-2412	Work at home. Flextime. Compressed work weeks. Part-time.	Funds community child care programs. Supports before/after school and holiday programs and summer camps. Back-up care. R&R. Sick child days.	Resource and referral.	Long-term care insurance. Savings plan. Stock ownership/purchase plan. Scholarships. Family leave, one year with job back. Phase-back for new moms. Adoption aid.
Barnett Banks Laura Street Jacksonville, FL 32202	Work at home. Job sharing. Flextime. Compressed work weeks. Part-time.	On-site/near-site center. Supports before/after school and holiday programs, summer camp, and sick care. R&R. Sick child days.	Resource and referral.	Profit sharing. Savings plan. Stock ownership/purchase plan. On-site fitness centers. Phase-back for new moms.
Corning Houghton Park Corning, NY 14831	Work at home. Job sharing. Flextime. Compressed work weeks. Part-time.	3 near-site centers. Supports before/after school and holiday programs and summer camp. Back-up care. R&R. Sick child days.	Fairs. Seminars. Support groups.	Long-term care insurance. Profit sharing. Savings plan. Stock ownership/purchase plan. Phase-back for new moms. Adoption aid.
Fel-Pro 7450 N. McCormick Boulevard Skokie, IL 60076	Work at home. Job sharing. Flextime. Compressed work weeks. Part-time.	On-site center. Funds community child care programs. Summer camp. Supports back-up care, in-home sick care. Sick child days.	Resource and referral.	Profit sharing. Scholarships. On-site fitness center. Phase-back for new moms. Adoption aid. Gifts.

Source: Based on information from Milton Moskowitz and Carol Townsend, "100 Best Companies for Working Mothers," *Working Mother* (October 1993), 27–66.

Table 1.1 (continued)
1993 *Working Mother's* 10 Best Companies

| | | *Family-Friendly Options* | | |
Companies	Flexible Work Options	Child Care	Elder Care	Benefits
Glaxo 5 Moore Drive Research Triangle Park, NC 27709	Job sharing. Flextime. Compressed work weeks. Part-time.	2 on-site centers. Funds community child care programs, before/after school programs, and summer camp. Reimburses for costs during nonroutine travel. R&R. Sick child days.	Resource and referral.	Profit sharing. Savings plan. Scholarships. On-site fitness center. Breast pumps. Phase-back for new moms. Adoption aid.
IBM Old Orchard Road Armonk, NY 10504	Work at home. Flextime. Part-time.	Funds/support community child care programs and before/after school, holiday, and summer programs. Supports back-up care. R&R.	Resource and referral.	Long-term care insurance. Profit sharing. Savings plan. Stock ownership/purchase plan. Scholarships. Phase-back for new moms. Adoption aid.
Johnson & Johnson 1 Johnson & Johnson Plaza New Brunswick, NJ 08933	Work at home. Job sharing. Flextime. Part-time.	3 on-site centers. Supports a near-site center. Funds community child care programs. Summer program. R&R. Sick child days.	Resource and referral.	Long-term care insurance. Savings plan. Stock ownership/purchase plan. Scholarships. On-site fitness center. Phase-back for new moms. Adoption aid. Stock options.
NationsBank 100 N. Tyron Street Charlotte, NC 28255	Work at home. Job sharing. Flextime. Part-time.	Near-site center. Back-up care. Child care subsidies. R&R. Sick child days.		Savings plan. Stock ownership/purchase plan. Scholarships. Phase-back for new moms. Adoption aid. Stock options.

Table 1.1 (continued)
1993 *Working Mother's* 10 Best Companies

| Companies | Family-Friendly Options | | | |
	Flexible Work Options	Child Care	Elder Care	Benefits
St. Paul Companies 385 Washington Street St. Paul, MN 55102	Work at home. Job sharing. Flextime. Compressed work weeks. Part-time.	On-site center. Funds/supports community child care, before/after school, and holiday programs. Reimburses for nonroutine travel. R&R. Sick child days.		Tuition reimbursement. Savings plan. Stock ownership/purchase plan. Breast pumps. Phase-back for new moms.
Xerox P.O. Box 1600 Stamford, CT 06904	Work at home. Job sharing. Flextime. Compressed work weeks. Part-time.	Funds community child care programs. Before/after school, holiday, and summer programs. Supports back-up care. Subsidizes sick care. R&R. Sick child days.	Resource and referral.	Profit sharing. Savings plan. Scholarships for employee's children. Phase-back for new moms. Adoption aid.

about child care issues in new ways. Times have changed, and George realizes that Alison has had experiences that are vastly different from those of his wife, Marilyn. He understands that Alison's career is important to her, and that she is highly respected for her knowledge and experience in corporate law. Are there viable ways for a talented young woman to continue working while caring for a young child? What will be the impact of a new baby on his son-in-law's architectural practice, still struggling through recessionary times? What is quality child care anyway? Is a live-in nanny hard to find? Is a live-in nanny the best option? At the same time, George finds himself reflecting on his company, his employees, and the last senior executive meeting. Child care came up in various contexts. Could it be that the media hype on family-friendly policies—articles he only scans unthinkingly—have some validity? Could it be that *child care is a major issue of the '90s*?

WHY ARE SO MANY COMPANIES THINKING ABOUT CHILD CARE?

There are four major reasons:

1. The demographics of the work force have changed dramatically since the 1950s, when traditional benefits packages were organized.
2. Companies' attitudes toward employees are changing, away from "just do your job" toward a desire for employee input and shared responsibility.
3. The bottom-line payoffs of family-friendly policies are being analyzed more closely.
4. The nation's concern over the declining academic achievement of its young people is focusing attention on children and stimulating collaborative efforts among businesses, schools, communities, and parents.

Changes in the Work Force

The last three decades have been years of major cultural, social, and economic change. Families are changing, the labor force is changing, and the workplace is changing. Adaptation to change has become a primary competency for both organizations and the people that are part of them.

There is an immense difference between the traditional American worker and the modern one. Today women make up nearly half of the work force. That means that the traditional image of family—Dad with the briefcase, Mom in the kitchen—is fading fast. Between the mid-1980s and the year

2000, the bulk of new entrants into the workplace (82 percent) will be women, nonwhites, and immigrants. Demographers have predicted that 64 percent of all workers in 2005 will be women.[7] In the early 1990s, women are earning 52 percent of undergraduate degrees and 50 percent of graduate degrees; half of all MBA students are women.[8]

Companies are already beginning to compete for a diverse labor pool, a labor pool that is shrinking. Predictions are that by 1995 the bank of potential employees will drop 24 percent from the 1980 level. In the 1950s, population growth was 1.9 percent per year. By the year 2000, it is expected to have fallen to 0.7 percent per year. Effects are already being felt.[9] A 1990 Towers Perrin and Hudson Institute survey reported that 65 percent of companies were already facing labor shortages.[10] During recent recessionary times, the demand for employees has diminished, but, as the economy picks up, the reduced labor pool will again be felt.

A look into American homes also finds evidence of dramatic change. Fewer than 10 percent of the population lives in the classic family headed by a male breadwinner, and only 26 percent of American households consist of married couples with children.[11] Half of all mothers with children under one year are working, and by 1995 two-thirds of women with preschool children and three-quarters with school-age children are expected to be in the labor force. By the year 2000, potentially 81 percent of mothers will be working outside their homes.[12] In 1990, one out of every five children lived in a single-parent family. Stepchildren comprise 20 percent of all children of married couples. People living with nonrelatives make up the fastest-growing household type, rising 46 percent in the 1980s. The fastest-growing family type is the single-parent family headed by a father, which grew 34 percent in the past five years.[13]

Employers realize they are looking at a work force that is more diverse, more female, and made up of more dual-career families. (See Exhibit 1.1.) Companies are finding employees, men and women, who are struggling to be both responsible workers and responsive family members. Numbers of companies are taking steps toward building more family-friendly organizations. They are developing corporate family policies, creating task forces to identify specific problem areas, appointing work-family managers, and designing benefits for all phases of the life cycle. The goals are integrating work and family and improving work force productivity. As Robert Rosen says in *The Healthy Company,* "Much as the industrial revolution predominated in the 1900s and the information revolution captured the 1960s, the 1990s will be a time when the *human-resource revolution* takes center stage."[14] According to Michael Carey of J&J Personal Products Co., "There

Exhibit 1.1
The Changing Work Force

- Today, nearly half of the work force is made up of women.
- Eighty-two percent of the new entrants into the workplace in the 1990s will be women, nonwhite, and immigrants.
- Sixty-four percent of all workers in 2005 will be women.
- Half of all MBA students today are women.
- Less than 10 percent of the population today lives in a family headed by a male breadwinner whose wife remains at home to care for the children.
- Only 26 percent of households consist of married couples with children.
- Half of all mothers with children under one year are working.
- By 1995, 66 percent of women with preschool children and 75 percent of women with school-age children are expected to be in the labor force.
- By 2000, potentially 81 percent of all mothers will be working outside their homes.
- The fastest-growing family type is the single-parent family headed by a father.

is extremely heavy competition for good people these days. One of the ways to get and keep them is help them fulfill their family responsibilities."[15]

A June 1991 *Harvard Business Review* article summarizing the results of a worldwide survey of 12,000 corporate managers reported that managers are finding "walls crumbling"—walls between nations, walls between the company and the society in which it exists, walls between work and home, as well as walls that once divided managers from workers within the workplace itself. Demographic change in a worldwide market economy is influencing the thinking of managers everywhere:

> "A family friendly workplace will be central to corporate efforts to recruit and retain qualified labor."

> "We are entering a decade where flextime and child care will be viewed not as costly frills, but as mainstream investments that yield substantial rates of return."

"In the last decade of the twentieth century, human capital will become the prime source of wealth and power for individuals, corporations, and nations."

"The challenge for business is to develop an agenda that identifies ways to contribute to today's families and tomorrow's work force."[16]

Changes in the Workplace

Workplaces today are undergoing fundamental change. Some of the changes are technical. New technology, from computer technology and fax machines and information processing and management, is rapidly changing the way that business is done. Other changes are structural, as organizations downsize, reorganize, merge, and up-size.

Further changes can be seen in the managerial realm. Hierarchical management styles are giving way to participative models. Work is undertaken in more interdependent and less segmented ways. Companies today place a high priority on the value of teamwork. Employees, employee teams, and managers collaborate, forming partnerships where talents and skills are sometimes used to lead and sometimes used to follow.

Companies are examining issues of power and control and revamping organizational charts. Richard Semler, president of Semco S.A., for example, speaks of the need to topple the pyramid management style. "Pyramids emphasize power, promote insecurity, distort communications, hobble interaction, and make it very difficult for people who plan and the people who execute to move in the same direction."[17]

People are being valued as a company's most important asset. Although such phrases are frequently seen in mission statements and are often considered standard public relations copy, some companies are reworking their entire organization around "new people concepts." Donald E. Petersen, chairman of Ford until 1990, identified the source of decline at Ford as a "people" problem, not foreign competitors. "We needed to change the 'now hear this' mentality, the notion that an employee should listen carefully and not think too much." Rigid control at Ford and many other companies has been replaced with leadership that empowers employees, where responsibility and authority are shared. Teams share power and leadership. The change began at Ford in small ways. Managers met with employees, asked for their suggestions, and listened. This process resulted in two new programs, Employee Involvement and Participative Management, as well as a new mission statement, which states, "involvement and teamwork are our core human values."[18]

This greater emphasis on teamwork naturally leads to an analysis of how to help each member of the team become more effective and productive. If child care and family-related problems affect one member of a team, they may well affect the entire team. This phenomenon has shown up in numerous focus groups and surveys that we have performed for companies:

> "I do not have any children, but I feel that [the lack of quality child care] is an important problem and would be willing to contribute to make [quality child care] available."
>
> "Even though I have no kids, I would forgo some of my benefits since I am adversely affected by others' child care problems."
>
> "The priorities here are mixed up. They want quality work, but they don't take into account family matters. People can't concentrate with all the stress."
>
> "It happens quite often that we have to cover for other people's child care problems. It puts a strain on supervisors and other workers."

Stride Rite CEO Arnold Hiatt considers the intergenerational Stride Rite dependent care center an investment in teamwork. "For me, it's an economic investment. To the extent that you can help your colleagues with their problems, you integrate them onto the team and you have an advantage over your competition."[19] At John Hancock Financial Services, Senior Vice President of Human Resources Diane Capstaff says, "Even though we personally may not feel the burden of child care, we work with people each day who do. We want to work with the best qualified and most productive people that we can. To the extent that we can put some policies and programs in place that will assist our employees in being more productive, we are all winners."[20]

There are, however, some who question the equity of child care programs. A *Wall Street Journal* supplement on June 21, 1993, "What about Us? Family Support Programs May Have a Side Effect: Resentment among Childless Workers," reported on this possibility. According to a Hewitt Associates survey of 14,000 workers, 20 percent of employees complain that coworkers with children are unfairly singled out for help.[21] Many companies are addressing this complaint with the development of new programs, as child care becomes just one facet of work-life policy. Xerox, for example, implemented life-cycle benefits in 1993 that allow employees to request up to $10,000 during the course of their career in extra taxable income to help pay for family expenses. The program begins with a child care subsidy, but Xerox has plans to add subsidies for other family-related expenses such as college tuition, elder care, and mortgage payments for first-time home buyers.

Benefits to the Company

In the spring of 1993, two studies were released that were unusually comprehensive in analyzing the benefits to a corporation of family-oriented programs. The Johnson & Johnson study, conducted by Families and Work Institute, and the University of Chicago's Fel-Pro study indicated that employees who take advantage of benefits such as child care programs and flexible working hours perform better and are less likely to quit than employees who do not. When the studies were released at a joint press conference, Chris Kjeldsen, vice president of human resources at Johnson & Johnson, and Paul Legman, president of Fel-Pro, said they had no precise figures on the programs' financial impact but noted that the reduced turnover and increased productivity recorded in the studies meant long-term advantages for their companies. "We feel good about these policies," Legman said, "but above all we do them because our business requires us to be competitive." Employees who use work-family benefits at Fel-Pro were found to be more likely to take part in quality-improvement efforts and team problem solving. The *Washington Post* noted that the fact that the two companies are quite different in size (Johnson & Johnson has 39,000 employees; Fel-Pro, 2,000) is also significant as an indicator of the broad appeal these kinds of programs can have.[22] At Johnson & Johnson, two years after the introduction of the work-family program employees reported that their jobs interfered less with their family lives. This reduction of stress in balancing work and family at Johnson & Johnson has occurred despite the fact that the average employee worked longer hours at a more demanding job in 1992 than in 1990.[23]

These studies are the first among many current efforts to look at the costs and benefits of family-friendly programs; others are underway as this book goes to press. Work-family programs are moving out of the arena of "soft benefits" and are being considered with more precise cost-benefit analysis. The U.S. Department of Labor is funding grants for such studies, and the number of firms conducting analyses using specific statistical or actuarial data, while still small, is growing. Research in the field over the next several years will focus on correlations between work-family programs and improvements in a company's bottom line. As the full range of family-friendly benefits is studied, the effects of child care benefits specifically will also be examined more closely.

Thus far, there is only a small body of research available related to child care programs' benefits to companies. Very few firms have evaluated their child care initiatives. The research that does exist, however, suggests that child care centers, along with parental leave policies and flextime, do offer returns to companies. A Conference Board summary of more than 80 studies conducted before 1991 indicates that reduced turnover and improved recruitment are the most significant benefits of employer-supported child care centers.[24] J. Douglas Phillips of Merck & Company has analyzed return on investment in a child care center from turnover savings only.[25]

A realization that "virtually all corporate activities are screened through a productivity lens" led Boston University's Center on Work and Family to explore, through a 1991 Ford Foundation grant, the relationship between family dependent care and productivity. Authors of a monograph that grew out of a 1990 conference with participants from psychology, sociology, economics, demography, and business administration presented a comprehensive review of the literature in a report entitled *Linking the Worlds of Family and Work: Family Dependent Care and Workers' Performance.* While addressing the limitations in recent research, such as the lack of longitudinal data, the report highlighted some consistent findings. One finding is the pervasiveness of stress experienced by employees who are struggling to balance family and work responsibilities. Another is that employers and supervisors who have been surveyed consistently praise the impact of corporate-sponsored child care programs on employee morale and job satisfaction.

Additionally, both survey and experimental research generally support the notion that on-site child care reduces working parents' absenteeism and tardiness. Finally, though the evidence is still considered tentative due to a need to develop more sophisticated measures, there is evidence to suggest that on-site care may positively impact employees' performance and have positive effects on employee turnover. The literature, thoroughly reviewed in this report, consistently documents that employees do not leave worries and concerns about dependent care behind when they enter the workplace. In its summary, the report notes that available studies use outcome measures that tap quality of work life (such as morale and stress) and withdrawal measures (such as absenteeism, tardiness, and turnover) rather than output measures (such as quantity, quality, or efficiency).[26] The Johnson & Johnson study and the Fel-Pro study are among the first to report in this latter realm of output measures. One longitudinal study, completed in 1994 for a large suburban hospital, did find that employees with children in an on-site child care center were better performers, had less turnover, and were absent less than employees with children elsewhere. However, employees with no children were more committed and involved with their jobs than employees with children.[27]

Some companies, however, are not interested in gathering statistics of cost effectiveness. Ben Cohen and Jerry Greenfield of Ben & Jerry's Homemade admit that they do not think they are going to be able to particularly measure the effects of their child care center in dollars and cents. "You can't find out exactly how much extra productivity you get from people if their children are well taken care of. We want to keep people happy at the job."[28] Steve Bloomfield, human services director of Fel-Pro, said in an *Employee Services Management* article, "How do you measure the sense of relief a father has because he knows his boy is at Summer Camp and not . . . on the streets of the city?"[29]

According to the Conference Board, sufficient evidence exists to convince employers that work-family programs can positively affect the bottom line. Gaps in the research will be filled in the next several years as "a new generation of research calls for greater sophistication in process and purpose—inquiries that are interdisciplinary, longitudinal, comparative, and visionary."[30] These efforts are predicted to bring the evidence some companies still require before they get involved.

The Future Work Force

Another force, operating in tandem with the cost-benefit issue, is pushing corporate-sponsored child care programs forward: companies are beginning to worry about the quality of the work force in the future. Business leaders are beginning to understand that education begins at birth. The care and education that very young children receive before they enter kindergarten directly affects their success in school. We cannot put young children into care situations where they are ignored much of the time and expect them to thrive. This, of course, is the premise behind Head Start, but Head Start does not reach many children. Dr. Edward F. Zigler of the Yale Bush Center in Child Development and Social Policy asserts that 70 percent of the child care in this country is of poor quality, and that it is mostly middle-class children who are victims of this poor-quality care. According to Zigler, whether you look at the weakness of the regulations or directly observe the programs, you will come up with a figure of about 70 percent poor-quality care.[31] In April 1994 the Carnegie Corp. released a study citing the fact that many children under age three live in poverty and are placed in low-quality child care. The study also reported new scientific evidence of the importance of the proper early environment to brain development.[32] Also released in April 1994 was a study of family day care by Families and Work Institute. Only 9 percent of the homes surveyed provided "good quality care." More than one-third of the home programs were considered to be so poor that they were "potentially harmful to the child's healthy growth."[33]

Owen Butler, retired CEO of Procter & Gamble, speaks for many enlightened business leaders when he says, "The best way for business to invest in educating the disadvantaged is to reach them early. By age five, they're already so deprived they can't benefit from schooling. It took us years to develop Tartar-Control Crest, years to make a profit on our investment. So we understand the economics of early childhood programs."[34]

Evidence of the business community's concern for the nation's early childhood education system is visible on several fronts. A coalition of executives from Fortune 500 companies, the Committee for Economic Development (CED), calls for partnerships to work toward improved coordination between government, community, and business efforts. In the foreword to *Education Before School: Investing in Quality Child Care*, a CED publication, Robert E. Campbell, vice chairman of Johnson & Johnson, acknowledges the committee's strong belief in the investment in human resources as an essential element of a strong and competitive economy. "Child care is more than a place where parents can safely leave their children during the workday. As a vital part of the nation's education system, it is a place where our youngest children can begin to develop the fundamental skills that allow them to become lifelong learners and productive workers and citizens. . . . Child care is an important service for families and employers. Reliable and affordable care allows parents to work more productively."[35]

Business leaders know that the economy of the twenty-first century will call for new skills. Developing a competitive world-class work force requires efforts *now* to invest in the earliest years of children's lives. Another important effort from business leaders who understand this need is the American Business Collaboration for Quality Dependent Care (ABC Collaborative), approximately 145 companies working together since 1992 to improve the quality and supply of child care services nationwide. Many of the nation's leading corporations have joined together to pledge $26.8 million to the project. As of April 1993, 300 initiatives were supported by ABC, with 58 up and running.[36]

Richard B. Stolley, editorial director of Time and president of the Child Care Action Campaign, believes that American business must work to change public policy on behalf of families and children. "We should not expect businesses to be social revolutionaries . . . but we cannot make important social progress in this country without the help, or at least the permission, of business. Helping families succeed is not a revolutionary act for business, but one of purest conservatism." [37] The Child Care Action Campaign and the Council of Chief State School Officers have joined forces in another movement to help ensure that all child care situations are places where children will learn and develop appropriately.

Robert Reich, secretary of labor, in a 1992 speech to the Children's Defense Fund conference, emphasized that education begins at birth, not at age six. He made it clear that child care is indeed a business issue, and that high-quality programs are essential to the education and preparation of the next generation of workers.[38]

It is a relatively well-known fact that employer-sponsored child care programs are among the best-quality programs in the country, often showcases for companies. The chapters ahead will highlight why this is so. Businesses know that the programs they sponsor will reflect back on the company, and most want their child care programs to display the same quality as the rest of the company. Companies concerned about quality, however, sometimes struggle with how to identify and define quality centers. According to a 1993 Catalyst report, *Child Care in Corporate America: Quality Indicators and Model Programs,* companies tend to "reinvent the wheel." They need guidance in identifying models that are not necessarily frequently reported on in the media; in understanding what questions to ask and which consultants to rely on, if any; and in dealing with multisite situations.[39]

There are public-private partnership movements mushrooming across the country that are aimed at educating both parents and employers on the characteristics of quality child care. One such partnership is Child Care Aware, sponsored by Dayton Hudson Foundation, Mervyn's, and Target Stores, in cooperation with the National Association for the Education of Young Children, the National Association for Family Day Care, the National Association of Child Care Resource and Referral Agencies, and the Child Care Action Campaign. Child Care Aware's goal is to highlight and focus attention on the characteristics of quality child care.

Quality is a major theme of this book. It will be the primary point of convergence for decision making and for discussion in each of the chapters to follow. A pamphlet from Child Care Aware says, "Quality child care can make a big difference in the future of your child, your community, even the world." Executives and CEOs who have been in the vanguard of corporate-supported child care understand the magnitude of this commitment to children and to our culture. In 1988, before the Select Committee on Children, Youth, and Families of the U.S. House of Representatives, Harry Freeman, executive vice president of American Express, talked about the big picture:

> Corporations don't do business in a vacuum. They do business in communities. That's where our employees and customers and shareholders live. So helping communities is good for business and vice versa. Call it altruism. Call it enlightened self-interest. Call it common sense . . . or good business. Corporations have an obligation to the communities, and one important measure of a community's well-being is the quality of the facilities it provides for its children. . . . I don't have to be Dr. Spock to tell you that the learning, working, and socializing habits of a lifetime are formed in early childhood. . . . In an era where the dual-income or single-parent household is the rule, that guidance must be aided by high-quality child care. The cost of improving our child care capabilities will be high, I can assure you. But the cost of not doing this is prohibitive—both in terms of our future quality of life and sheer ability to compete. That's my bottom-line message for today![40]

You can be sure that when George Oliver initiates a child care center for his employees, he will insist that the children receive the best care possible.

NOTES

1.   Jay Matthews, "Easing an Employee's Family Strains Reaps Benefits for Employers Too," *Washington Post,* May 2, 1993.

2.   Families and Work Institute, *An Evaluation of Johnson & Johnson's Balancing Work and Family Program, Executive Summary* (New York: Families and Work Institute, 1993), 4–10.

3.   Interview with Admiral J. William Kime, commandant, U.S. Coast Guard, September 1, 1993.

4.   Jolie Solomon, "Companies Try Measuring Cost Savings from New Types of Corporate Benefits," *Wall Street Journal,* December 29, 1988, Marketplace.

5.   Sue Shellenbarger, "Work & Family: So Much Talk, So Little Action," *Wall Street Journal,* June 21, 1993, R4.

6.   Ellen Galinsky and Dana Friedman, *Education Before School: Investing in Quality Child Care* (New York: Scholastic Press, 1993), 125.

7.   Ibid., 15.

8.   Felice N. Schwartz, *Breaking with Tradition: Women and Work, the New Facts of Life* (New York: Warner Books, 1992), 137.

9.   Galinsky and Friedman, *Education Before School,* 15.

10. Robert H. Rosen, *The Healthy Company* (New York: Putnam Publishing Group, 1991), 242.

11. Ibid., 266.

12. Committee for Economic Development, *Why Child Care Matters: Preparing Children for a More Productive America* (New York: Committee for Economic Development, 1993), 5.

13. Rosen, *Healthy Company,* 266.

14. Ibid., 300.

15. Ibid., 288.

16. Rosabeth Moss Kanter, "Transcending Business Boundaries: 12,000 World Managers View Change," *Harvard Business Review* (May–June 1991), 151–64.

17. Rosen, *Healthy Company,* 71.

18. Ibid., 72–73.

19. Barbara Kantrowitz and Lauren Picker, "Day Care: Bridging the Generation Gap," *Newsweek* (July 16, 1990).

20. Jan Mason, "Child Care Is a Growing Concern: Corporate Kids," *New York Times Magazine* (March 18, 1990).

21. Laurie M. Grossman, "What about Us?" *Wall Street Journal,* June 21, 1993.

22. Matthews, "Easing an Employee's Family Strains."

23. Families and Work Institute, *An Evaluation,* 10.

24. The Conference Board, *Linking Work-Family Issues to the Bottom Line* (New York: The Conference Board, 1991).

25. J. Douglas Phillips, "Economic Justification of Child Care Initiatives" (paper presented at Association of Child Care Consultants International conference, Anaheim, CA, November 9, 1993).

26. Bradley K. Googins, Judith G. Gonyea, and Marcie Pitt-Catsouphes, *Linking the Worlds of Family and Work: Family Dependent Care and Workers' Performance* (Boston: Boston University, Center on Work & Family, December 1990), 31–32.

27. Debra J. Cohen and Rodger W. Griffeth, "Evaluating the Effectiveness of an On-Site Employer Sponsored Child Care Center: Human Resource Implications" (April 1994) (unpublished manuscript).

28. Bonnie Neugebauer, "From Cherries Garcia to Child Care—The Story of Ben & Jerry's Children's Center," *Exchange Magazine* (November/December 1990), 41.

29. *Employee Services Management* (November 1991).

30. The Conference Board, *Linking Work-Family Issues,* 58.

31. Edward Zigler, "Child Care and Education: The Critical Connection" (speech at 1992 Child Care Action Campaign conference, New York, NY).

32. Barbara Vobejda, "6 Million of Nation's Youngest Children Face Developmental Risks," *Washington Post,* April 13, 1994, A3.

33. Barbara Vobejda, "Family Day Care 'Barely Adequate,' " *Washington Post,* April 8, 1994, A1.

34. Rosen, *Healthy Company,* 163.

35. Galinsky and Friedman, *Education Before School,* ix.

36. "American Business Collaboration Running Ahead of Schedule," *The National Report on Work and Family,* April 27, 1993, 1.

37. Karol L. Rose, *Work and Family: Program Models and Policies* (New York: John Wiley & Sons, 1993), vi.

38. Robert Reich, "Building Blocks for Change: The Roles of Institutions and Networks in Transforming Society for Children and Families" (speech at annual Children's Defense Fund conference, Washington, DC, March 11, 1993).

39. Catalyst, *Child Care in Corporate America: Quality Indicators and Model Programs* (New York: Catalyst, 1993), 10.

40. Harry L. Freeman, "The Corporate Stake in Child Care" (testimony before the Subcommittee on Children, Family, Drugs and Alcoholism, United States Senate, March 15, 1988).

Chapter Two

■ ■ ■ ■ ■

Child Care Choices: "Multitudes in the Valley of Decision"

Bob Roman listened intently to the reports of his senior H.R. managers. Sharon Klein was making some good points.

"We've been doing some research, Bob, and it looks like we have several options other than a child care center. Some companies are providing child care referrals for their employees; others are giving financial vouchers to their employees so they can better afford their child care. We think we need to spend some more time doing a really thorough research job to see what our options are and to find the simplest way for us to solve our problems."

"I agree with Sharon that we need to know our options, Bob, but we also have to know what our problems are. What are we trying to solve? I'd like to research child care need surveys and work on developing one for us."

"Good point, Sam. You and Sharon have done some excellent thinking. Go forward and let's meet again in two weeks. Remember, if we actually end up initiating something, it will obviously affect the whole company, so if you need informa-

tion or feedback from people in other departments, let me know and I'll arrange it. I hope you can take care of this research in addition to everything else you're doing, because you have to." Bob smiled.

"Nooo problem, Bob." Sam smiled back as he and Sharon got up to leave.

WHAT ARE OUR CHILD CARE OPTIONS?

In many situations, there is only one right solution to a problem. If you have a car that won't start, the mechanic needs to find the exact solution— maybe it's the ignition system, maybe the battery, maybe the timing. But with child care, there often are several potential solutions, and you can choose the ones that work best in your particular corporate culture, in your community, and within your budgetary constraints. You still have to match solutions to your company's particular problems, but there are usually several workable alternatives.

Potential solutions fall into six major categories:

1. Provision of direct services
2. Alternative work schedules
3. Financial assistance
4. Education and resources
5. Community assistance
6. Other creative options

Direct Services

There are several types of direct child care services a company can provide:

- On-site/near-site child care centers
- Consortia child care centers
- School-age child care programs
- Emergency back-up child care centers
- Family child care provider networks
- Sick-child care programs
- Weekend/evening child care
- Transportation services

Let's look at these direct service options in some detail.

On-Site/Near-Site Child Care Centers. No option is quite as publicity-generating as the on-site or near-site child care center. An on-site or near-site child care center is sponsored by the employer and is located at or near the work site. The center can be run by the employer itself or by a separate child care corporation.

Centers can be designed to operate during the hours when child care services are most needed and to serve children of any age: infants, toddlers and two-year-olds, three- to five-year-old children, and elementary school-age children. There is a nationwide shortage of care for children under two years old, so this is one area of special need. Centers can operate full-time and/or part-time programs. Full-service child care centers make the most fiscal sense when there are a large number of employees who will use the center. Companies with a smaller need sometimes find it beneficial to develop small emergency back-up programs, where parents can bring their children when their usual child care arrangements fall through for the day.

Most employers pay the costs of developing child care centers, as well as ongoing costs associated with the space, such as utilities and landscaping fees. Many employers also subsidize their centers to make centers affordable to most employees. Some employers finance scholarships or sliding fee scales so that the center is affordable to all. Finances, budgets, and taxes will be discussed in detail in chapter 6.

Centers must be licensed by states and sometimes localities. In chapter 5 we will discuss the legal and liability issues that give some corporate executives pause, along with a whole range of options for running a center.

BE&K Engineering and Construction has brought the concept of an on-site child care center to a new height. BE&K spent $750,000 to build a mobile center than can shuttle from site to site to accommodate construction workers on the job.[1]

Consortia Child Care Centers. Consortia child care centers are a good option for companies that do not have enough of a child care need to warrant their own centers (chapter 4 explains how to determine this) and are located near other companies that are also interested in child care centers. In a consortium, several companies band together to develop a new child care center, and the center is incorporated as a separate entity from the participating companies. The companies provide start-up funding and may provide scholarship money to the center. If the center is open to the general community, usually the employees of participating companies have priority for placement of their children in the center.

The advantage of a consortium is that the center's costs and liabilities are shared among the participating companies. Tom Grubisich, publisher of *The Connection* newspaper and president of the Reston Area Child Care Consortium in northern Virginia, says, "The consortium provides an opportunity for businesses to get involved in child care. The consortium model provides the necessary liability insulation and, for us, was a vehicle that many corporations were willing to hop on to."[2]

In a consortium, however, the space available for children of employees of each participating company may be limited. Also, each company will have less influence over policy issues and quality than it would have if the center served only its employees, and it may be difficult to get companies to agree on policies.

School-Age Child Care Programs. Some companies find that their best option is to concentrate on programs for children ages five through 12. As the 1993 *National Study of Before and After School Programs* reported, it is estimated that by 1995 more than three-fourths of all school-age children—over 25 million American youngsters—will have mothers in the work force.[3] There is a critical need for school-age child care programs. The demand for such programs far outweighs the supply, and this is an issue that concerns employers, policymakers, and child care advocates.

The time that children spend outside the classroom has great influence on their lives. Many of the formal and informal activities that occupy the hours and days that school is not in session, such as participating in scout troops, taking music lessons, and playing outdoors with friends, depend upon a stay-at-home parent to plan or oversee the activities or at least to provide transportation. Children today have the same essential needs as earlier generations for leisure activities and social interaction with peers, but often these activities must occur in a more structured setting because there is no parent at home at 3:00 with a glass of milk and a plate of cookies. A well-planned school-age child care program can meet the child's needs well and, at the same time, allow mom and dad to concentrate on their work.

School-age programs can include before- and after-school programs, programs for school holidays, and summer programs, and they can be located in schools, in child care centers, in recreation centers, in family day-care homes, or at the work site. The key to operating school-age programs is *collaboration*. There are organizations in most communities that have experience operating programs for five- to 12-year-olds, and most of these organizations would be delighted to work in tandem with a corporation. Investigate Boys and Girls Clubs, YMCAs, religious organizations, chambers of commerce, departments of Parks and Recreation, local child care centers, and especially elementary schools.

Collaborations on school-age programs can work for small as well as large corporations. A good model of a public-private partnership for providing child care during school vacations and summer has been established at Marriott International headquarters in Montgomery County, Maryland. Marriott provides meeting space, snacks, and some funding for the program, and the Montgomery County Recreation Department provides the staff and sets the curriculum.

The cost to companies is usually much less to develop a school-age program than to develop a full-service child care center because the space requirements are much reduced. Also, school-age programs can solve the "3:00 syndrome," when employees tie up phones to call home to check on children, or children call parents to report in. School-age programs are less expensive for parents than are programs for younger children.

Transportation problems inherent in moving children between child care sites and school must be addressed when developing a program. The "Transportation Services" section of this chapter discusses these problems.

For companies that have employees living in many different far-flung areas, a centralized before- and after-school program will not be a useful option, but vacation and summer programs may be most welcome. The St. Petersburg Times created a school-age holiday camp for employees' children and teamed up with a local children's museum to offer programs and field trips. The St. Paul Companies launched the Twin Cities' First Summer School-Age Child Care Seminar and Fair in March 1993.[4]

Some companies have actually started their own schools for employees' children. Of course these schools are open for the whole work day, and the holiday schedule follows that of the company. G.T. Water Products, a California manufacturing company with just 26 employees, provides a free on-site private year-round school program for employees' children, who range from kindergarteners to 12-year-olds. Hewlett-Packard teamed up with local officials to open an elementary school at its plant in Santa Rosa, California.

Other less extensive services can also help school-age children. Some companies purchase school-age activity kits for children of employees who are home alone after school.[5] Other companies set up a "warm-line" for employees' children to call if they have problems, are lonely, or need help with homework. Corporations that currently have on-site or near-site child care centers are beginning to add school-age programs to current programs in order to serve an even larger segment of the employee population.

Emergency Back-Up Child Care Centers. Emergency back-up child care centers are a popular option because they are less expensive to develop than full-service child care centers, and they clearly increase employee productivity. These centers are used only when the parent's regular child care arrangements fall through, such as when the baby-sitter is sick or the housekeeper does not arrive. This type of child care, which is sometimes called "emergency child care," "back-up child care," or "drop-in child care," can be sponsored by a single corporation or a consortium.

An emergency back-up child care program can be part of a full-service child care center or it can be run as a small center that employees may use only on an emergency basis. Although these centers are usually small, it is important that they be planned as carefully as full-scale child care centers. Emergency back-up child care centers must meet all applicable laws for physical design and program policy, and policies and procedures must be detailed in writing for parents and staff. Most of the issues that are relevant to the development of a full-service child care center are also relevant to the development of an emergency back-up child care center, so we will talk about back-up centers throughout the book. There are some issues, however, that are unique to back-up child care.

Necessary policies for emergency back-up child care centers relate to cancellations, arrivals, and limitations on use. If a back-up center is to be financially self-supporting, a cancellation policy is essential. Because such centers are small, every daily fee that is expected is needed. If a reservation is canceled within a specified time frame, it may not be necessary to charge a fee, but it is a good idea to charge the regular fee for "no-shows." Policies should also be set for arrival. Of course, all children must be pre-enrolled in order to attend, but parent schedules and phone numbers should be checked on the day the child attends. The center also needs policies to protect it from overuse. If the same 10 parents are always reserving spaces, the rest of the employees will not have as great an opportunity to utilize the service. It must be clear that the center is only for emergency care and only for the care of well children. Unless your center has been developed with a sick-child care component (and meets all applicable regulations for this), policies and procedures must protect the center from use by parents with sick children.

On-site emergency back-up child care centers have been a popular benefit for law firms to develop. For example, Bingham, Dana & Gould, a Boston law firm, jointly sponsors an emergency back-up child care center with two other Boston companies. The Federal National Mortgage Association (Fannie Mae) is an example of another company that has developed an on-site emergency back-up child care center. Fannie Mae's center serves its Washington, DC headquarters.

Another model of emergency back-up care is a program in New York City called Emergency Child Care Services. In this program, Child Care, Inc., a resource and referral agency in New York, contracts with businesses to provide care in employees' homes on an emergency back-up basis. The care is provided by home health aide agencies. Caregivers can be sent to employee homes if the child is mildly ill or if the child is well but the usual child care arrangements have fallen through for the day.

Some companies have also arranged for slots in regular community-based child care centers for company employees to use on an emergency back-up basis. Information on this option is given in the section "Vendor or Discount Systems" in this chapter.

Family Child Care Provider Networks. Family child care providers are people who take children into their homes for care. Often these people care for all ages of children, from infants through preschoolers, with some elementary school-age children arriving after 3:00. Parents often select this form of child care, especially for children under three and for school-age children. Multisite employers sometimes find networks an equitable way to address child care needs in their organization. Other companies take a consortium approach and create networks that are managed by local resource and referral agencies. America West Airlines in Phoenix and Las Vegas and Steelcase in Grand Rapids, Michigan, are both successfully working with networks; America West provides child care this way seven days a week, 24 hours a day.

Some family child care providers are licensed or certified, but many operate illegally or in a jurisdiction that does not require any type of licensure. Like center-based care, quality varies. There are wonderful family child care providers, but, as studies cited in chapter 1 have shown, many do not provide a properly nurturing experience for children. One option a business might consider would be to fund an existing child care center to develop a network of legally operated family child care homes, overseen by the child care center. It is very difficult for parents to assess the quality of care that their children receive in family child care homes, and there is certainly a need for child care provider training, which a company could fund. In exchange, the company would be developing a child care service that meets the needs of company employees. Selection, training, and supervision of providers are important issues for companies to consider when developing family child care provider networks. Companies should think in terms of their liability for the care provided in private homes.

Sick-Child Care Programs. Sick-child care programs are designed to care for mildly ill children of employees. They can be located in a child care center, a network of family child care homes, the child's own home with a visiting nurse, or a hospital setting.

There are very few sick-child care programs thus far in the country. Many states are only now in the process of writing regulations for sick-child care. In developing a sick-child care program, companies must ensure that policies and procedures are very carefully written to ensure quality and to protect against liability; it is best to care for only mildly ill children who appear to be on their way to recovery.

In a center-based program, the physical space must be specially designed with adequate plumbing and air-flow systems. Since parents are very reluctant to take their sick children to a strange environment for sick-child care, more workable options are to establish a sick bay in a well-child care center or to provide a program of in-home care. Some hospitals, like Children's National Medical Center in Washington, DC, offer a sick-child care service, in which trained health aides go to sick children's homes under contract to the parents' employers. The hospital program workers are usually licensed and bonded and are hospital employees. Some nanny services also offer in-home sick-child care, but they often will not assume any liability for the caregivers they send.

Often what employees value most is flexibility in company policies so they can stay home with their sick children. We talk about this need in the section "Alternative Work Schedules" later in this chapter.

Weekend/Evening Child Care. Some law firms have set up temporary child care programs to meet the needs of attorneys who work on weekends. Similarly, some accounting firms have established temporary child care programs to assist accountants who work long hours, especially during tax season. Companies that are interested in offering weekend or evening child care services must be careful about meeting local and state licensing laws.

Transportation Services. Transportation is a major problem, especially for parents of elementary school children. Suitable before- and after-school programs might exist, but often parents have no way to transport children to and from the programs because the parents must be working during those times. Companies might consider purchasing mini–school buses (which are available with seating for 16 to 20 children) to transport employees' children, or purchasing buses for existing school-age child care programs to use. Companies considering the purchase of mini–school buses must be sure the buses meet state and federal safety regulations for the transportation of children. School bus drivers must also meet state requirements. Companies might also work with community public schools to modify school bus routes so that children of employees can participate in school-age child care programs.

Alternative Work Schedules

Alternative work schedules provide the flexibility that many employees need and are another potential solution to employee and employer work-family problems. As Marcia Worthing of Avon Products has said, "Alternative scheduling will be necessary to attract the very best people. . . . Employees don't abuse the privilege, they just give you more in turn."[6] In 1991, the Conference Board surveyed work-family practitioners on flexibility and discovered the following:

- Successful pilot programs that are publicized help to overcome resistance.
- Reliable data on costs and employee needs are important, as is a communications strategy targeted to managers.
- Demographic information is important, but company-specific issues must be emphasized.
- Formal policies must be enhanced by supportive managers who are given flexibility in implementation.[7]

Alternative work schedules are an option that any company might consider, regardless of the company's size. Alternative work schedules include

- Flextime
- Telecommuting
- Personnel policy changes
- Job sharing
- Part-time work

Flextime. Flextime can be defined in various ways, depending upon the needs of your company. Some companies have core hours of 9:00 to 3:00, and employees can arrange with their supervisors to maintain an eight-hour day by coming in earlier or staying later in the afternoon. This type of schedule often helps employees with school-age children. Some companies allow employees to work four days of 10 hours each; others have a five-four-nine schedule possibility, which allows employees to work nine-hour days and have one weekday off every other week. These compressed work weeks give employees an extra day to spend with their children or to do chores and make appointments. Midday flex schedules allow employees to come in early and work late so that they can take extra time off midday (often to transport children from nursery schools to child care providers or to check on elderly relatives). Voluntary reduced-time schedules allow employees to work shorter hours for reduced pay.

Telecommuting. New technologies have enabled some companies to establish a policy of telecommuting. Telecommuting employees work at home for part of the workweek. Modems, E-mail, fax machines, and phones maintain the daily linkages to the office. As information and communication technology becomes more affordable, telecommuting is expected to grow; in recent years there has been much favorable press on the evolution of these programs. The standard "nine to five" schedule was designed around a traditional family that hardly exists anymore; telecommuting allows workers to work hours that suit their situations. While it is not a viable substitute for child care, telecommuting can offer workers the flexibility they need to handle some of the demands of dependent care responsibilities.

Some advantages of telecommuting are lower costs for office space and overhead, lower energy costs, fewer office distractions, and more flexibility for employees in managing work and family. Sometimes a satellite office cuts down on commuting time—on-call telecommuters can be at work in a matter of minutes. Telecommuting is becoming an attractive option, not only because it is family-friendly, but because it can provide employment for people with disabilities or people in rural situations. Telecommuting is also seen as part of the solution to traffic congestion and auto emission pollution. Training programs to educate managers and employees in this new way of working are considered critical to success. Managers must become comfortable supervising by objective rather than by hours worked.

Personnel Policy Changes. Personnel policies are evolving to meet the changing needs of the modern work force. Companies are refining leave policies, for example, to allow liberal leave in weather emergencies, leave for school conferences, and leave to volunteer or eat lunch in a child's school. Parental leave policies are also being revised, often to include gradual return to full-time work for new parents. Other policies that are aiding families are family-compatible shift schedules that are both predictable and flexible, telephone-access policies that accommodate important and necessary family calls, and advance warning of required travel so that parents can make arrangements for child care.

Some companies have changed their sick leave policies to personal leave policies so that employees can use leave time to stay home with sick children or attend to other personal business. Many employees have voiced unhappiness over having to lie to their supervisors in order to stay home with sick children, and this type of policy change eliminates that need. Some companies are looking at their "occurrence" policies to determine whether they are fair to working parents with young children who typically get sick often.

Job Sharing. Job sharing, in which two employees share the responsibilities of one full-time position, has worked well for some organizations. Job sharing often enables an organization to keep a valuable employee who otherwise might leave the company. In a job-sharing situation, employees can readily cover for one another for vacations, when there are family needs, and during illness. In order for job-sharing to succeed, employees need to be compatible, have effective communication skills, and have a real understanding of how to work as part of a team. In client-based firms, better service many result when two employees are aware of client needs. When functioning well, a shared job can give the position a wider range of skills and allow people to learn from one another.

Part-Time Work. Part-time work also serves the needs of some working parents. Recent surveys have found that many working parents would voluntarily switch to part-time schedules if available so they would have more time to spend with their families. Employees also stated that they would be more productive during work hours because their home responsibilities would be under better control.[8] A part-time work option may particularly benefit employers who have unusual work hours or high production quotas. Offering benefits to part-time employees can increase the retention of these employees.

Financial Assistance

Financial assistance programs include

- Voucher systems
- Vendor or discount systems
- Flexible spending accounts
- Baby bonuses
- Subsidies

Voucher Systems. Under a voucher system, an employer reimburses an employee for a portion of child care costs. The employer can limit the eligibility of employees to limit the expense of the program. For example, eligibility may be limited to lower-level employees or to employees with children under two years old. Levi Strauss & Co. is piloting a child care voucher program for employees whose family income is below $32,000 per year. Under the plan, these families can receive up to $100 per month per child for child care expenses.[9]

A voucher system makes child care more affordable to parents and leaves the choice of provider up to the parents. Also, a voucher system can be an effective recruitment tool. Temporary office-help agencies often recruit people with the announcement of child care vouchers. A variety of both small and large businesses, including J.C. Penney, have implemented voucher systems.

If the business pays for the vouchers, the cost may be tax deductible as an ordinary business expense. Some businesses have combined a voucher system with the establishment of a Dependent Care Assistance Program, set up under Section 129 of the IRS code, which allows employees to use pre-tax dollars for child care. Under a qualified benefits plan, the employer may also contribute up to $5,000 in child care expenses to the employee. This is generally not includable as taxable income to the employee.

Vendor or Discount Systems. In this type of arrangement, an employer purchases slots in a child care center and then resells them to employees, often at a discount. Or, an employer may negotiate a discount with a child care center and then offer employees who use the center a matching discount. Vendor or discount systems are sometimes used for emergency back-up child care. The CIGNA Companies, based in Philadelphia, offer discount programs at a number of child care centers near CIGNA offices and provide on-site child care at three locations. A vendor system helps make child care more affordable to employees, but because the employers choose the child care providers, it is possible that the slots arranged for by employers may not meet the needs of the employees.

Flexible Spending Accounts. With employer plans set up under Section 129 of the IRS Code, employees are able to pay for their child care expenses with pre-tax income. Several types of dependent care are usually covered in these plans, so that an employee can use pre-tax dollars to pay for child care or care for an elderly parent or dependent spouse. Since the income is set aside on a pre-tax basis, the employer does not have to pay FICA or FUTA on the money. Despite the tax advantages to both employer and employee, flexible spending accounts often have a low usage rate among lower-level employees, in part because of the IRS's "use it or lose it" rule. This rule requires employees who participate in flexible spending accounts to state in January the amount of salary to be withheld for the year. If they overestimate, they lose the money. In addition, lower-income people often have a hard time paying for child care with their reduced take-home pay, especially when they have to wait to be reimbursed. Another problem is that parents often use child care providers who will not release their social security numbers—a necessity for reimbursement.

There are, however, companies that have made major efforts to educate their employees about the benefits of flexible spending accounts and have a higher percentage of lower-income users. Jeffrey Hough, director of corporate citizenship at Calvert Group in Bethesda, MD, notes that participation in their Child Care Flexible Spending Account is as high among staff as it is among management. He believes that such high usage at the staff level stems from the thorough educational programs that Calvert provides to its employees: "Employees at all levels understand the tax benefits of this FSA and make an effort to make it work for them. Because child care expenses represent a larger percentage of our non-exempt employees' salary, they welcomed this benefit every bit as much as our higher paid managers."[10]

Baby Bonuses. Some smaller companies have instituted a system of "baby bonuses," in which new parents receive a bonus to help cover initial costs when a baby is born or adopted. Baby bonuses have taken the form of cash, stock, six months of diaper service, car seats, rocking chairs, and baby gifts.

Subsidies. Some companies subsidize child care costs for overtime work or for travel that requires employees to pay for additional child care. Other business travelers take their children along with them, and some hotels provide strollers, beepers, baby-sitters, and childproof rooms. Many conventions now include child care services on the program, and some companies pay for the cost of taking a child along. Stride Rite provides employees who have out-of-town assignments with a free referral service for nannies or child care, including reference checks. In this case, the employee pays for the cost of the care. There are companies, however, that reimburse all costs of child care for an employee on a business trip, including the cost of bringing a relative from a distant town to stay with the children (a grandparent, for example).

Education and Information

Employers may also provide education and information services. These services may take the form of

- Resource and referral systems
- Seminars, workshops, and support groups
- Resource fairs
- Resource centers
- Working-parent newsletters
- Supervisor training

Resource and Referral Systems. Resource and referral systems, or R & Rs, provide a computerized system to track child care openings that meet the specific needs of employees. There are national R & Rs as well as local ones. If an R & R receives public funding (and many do), its services are available free to individuals in the community. There are currently approximately 380 members of the National Association of Child Care Resource and Referral Agencies. Several national R & R businesses subcontract to these local groups for their clients who have nationwide businesses. Through a contract with an employer, many R & Rs will provide an "enhanced" service, which often includes verification of vacancies and follow-up phone calls to employees. R & Rs have also enhanced their services by providing seminars, counseling for teens, homework help, and adoption guidance, in addition to referrals for child care, elder care, and special needs care.

In order to avert negative publicity in the community when employees "use up" all the available family child care providers, employers often fund R & Rs to run recruitment campaigns to find new family child care providers. Recruitment efforts are also often undertaken to increase general availability in the community. An R & R system is only useful if there is an adequate supply of high-quality services available for referral. If parents cannot be referred to appropriate openings, or if the referrals are judged as low quality, the referral system will not serve its purpose and employees will not use it. Businesses can have a positive impact on the state of child care if they insist on a training component to any R&R service to enhance the quality of the service that employees' children receive.

Seminars, Workshops, and Support Groups. Some employers sponsor on-site seminar programs on parenting and care issues at times convenient for employees, such as during lunch hours. Popular topics include balancing work and family, choosing child care, commuting with your child, how to find school-age child care programs, how to find elder care services, and parenting issues such as discipline or developing children's self-esteem. Seminars are an inexpensive, yet a very helpful way for employers to demonstrate that they are concerned about work and family issues. Some companies have allowed paid release time for their employees to attend seminars and workshops.

Support groups for parents, and also for children of aging parents, are springing up in many companies. Many people can no longer access information from family and friends in the neighborhood because of time and distance problems, so finding support within the company is a major relief to employees. In support groups, employees share concerns, information, and solutions that have worked for them. These groups are a meaningful way to contribute to the reduction of employee stress. It is recommended that an experienced facilitator lead the groups.

Resource Fairs. At resource fairs, representatives of existing community programs and services can provide information to employees on resources that are available to help employees address caregiving and family needs. These fairs are held in a central location at the work site, usually for a two- or three-hour period in midday so that employees can visit the fair during their lunch break. A resource fair can benefit a broad range of employees and provides employees with one-stop shopping on community resources and services. Work and family fairs significantly enhance awareness of community resources and initiatives. Attendees can review self-selected literature, ask questions of exhibitors, and develop personal contacts with service providers. Familiarization with an agency or organization can be helpful to employees in problem solving or resolving crises at a later date.

Resource Centers. Companies can establish a permanent resource center or library to provide employees with information and resources on various topics, organizations, and issues of concern to them. Books, monthly magazines, educational videos, audiocassettes, newsletters, bibliographies, pamphlets and brochures, and filed articles can all be made available. Information on parenting, child and elder caregiving, intergenerational enrichment, available community services, speakers, and referral agencies may be included. A trained work-family resource coordinator can staff the resource center during certain hours to keep the collection up-to-date and to give individual attention to employees.

Since finding the time to locate needed information and programs is a tremendous problem for employees, the centralized resources in the work-site library are greatly appreciated. Often centers include areas to watch videos and bulletin boards with timely announcements. Resources important and relevant to seminars and support group meetings are often coordinated through the resource library.

Working-Parent Newsletters. Another way to distribute information to employees who are dealing with child care or elder care issues is through a newsletter distributed periodically. Companies can produce their own newsletters, which may be as simple as a one-pager describing work and family events at the company, giving some national work and family news, and including some articles specifically dealing with work and family issues, which would be helpful to employees with caregiving responsibilities. Some companies include a work and family column in their regular company newsletter. Alternatively, newsletters are produced commercially which companies can purchase and distribute to employees. Some excellent newsletters are

- *Work & Family Life*, a monthly newsletter published by Susan Ginsberg, formerly with Bank Street College. (212) 265-1282. Parenting and elder care articles as well as job-related articles are featured in this newsletter. Ellen Galinsky is the executive editor.
- *Education Today*, published eight times a year by the Educational Publishing Group. (617) 542-6500 or (800) 927-6006. The newsletter includes parenting information, advice and tips, and articles about education. The company logo can be put on the cover page of this newsletter.
- *Parent and Preschooler*, a monthly newsletter published by Betty Farber. (516) 742-9557. This source gives practical advice, suggestions, and resources to parents of preschoolers.

Supervisor Training. Training of both senior- and mid-level managers is essential to ensure that new programs and policies are implemented in a sensitive and supportive manner. When new policies are put into place, employees are often reluctant to take advantage of them because they fear repercussions from their supervisors. Supervisors may need to encourage employees to take advantage of new programs and policies. Formal work-and-family training sessions, particularly for managers, are gaining attention in many companies. When work-and-family benefits are in place but underutilized, it often indicates that supervisors need to learn how to translate policies into the everyday happenings of the workplace. Middle managers may not understand the need for these policies, because of their own experiences. If no one helped them balance work and family, they may be surprised to hear that they should be sympathetic and flexible. Supervisors are generally not vindictive, but sometimes they need to have further training in the new understandings of the workplace.

Training sessions usually focus on the business case for work-and-family programs—how programs relate to the bottom line—and on increasing awareness about managers' own perceptions of family-related issues. Internal demographics, the demographics of the national work force, a review of what other companies are doing, and a review of resources are also part of most trainings. It is essential that managers have a thorough understanding of the work-and-family programs that are in place. A major goal of manager training is to contribute to the creation of a workplace where managers and employees work together as a team to solve problems efficiently while keeping productivity high. We will talk more about supervisor training in chapter 11.

Community Investments

Companies can provide funding for the expansion or improvement of existing community programs that could benefit their own employees. Support may take the form of money, space, technical expertise, or in-kind services. For example, funding can be provided to lengthen a child care center's hours of program operation, for expansion or renovation of an existing facility, or for the development of an infant care program. Money can also be used for scholarships, teacher salary increases, equipment and materials purchases, staff or management training, or accreditation fees. (See chapter 4 for information on the national accreditation system for child care centers.) Resource and referral systems can use funds to recruit and train child care providers.

In some cases, funding goes to programs that have been recommended by employees. In others, companies use funds to attempt to fulfill community needs. Several large companies have established major funds to improve the quality and quantity of existing child care in the communities where many of their employees live. An example of such a fund is Levi Strauss's Levi's Child Care Fund, which gave grants in 1992 totaling $539,000 to expand and improve the quality of child care in four communities where it has plants.[11] Both large and small companies can adopt the fund concept. Child care programs will happily accept any amount of money to improve or expand their services. The ABC Collaborative mentioned in chapter 1 is one example of businesses joining together to establish a large fund.

Here are some valuable ways for a fund to invest in child care resources available in the community:

- Seed money for expansion of existing programs
- Recruitment campaigns for family child care providers
- Training money for family child care providers
- Technical assistance for child care centers for staff training, director training, or board development
- Scholarship money for children from lower-income families
- Money to begin a transportation program for school-age children to and from child care programs
- Accounting and legal assistance for child care programs
- Fund-raising assistance
- Salary subsidies for staff who stay on the job for a specified length of time to prevent staff turnover

Other Creative Options

Some companies have implemented very creative options that cost little and raise employee morale—new ones, in fact, are being devised all the time. For example, companies may give pagers to expectant fathers so that they can be contacted at any time. Some companies permit employees to bring infants to work, and others provide lactation rooms where nursing mothers can pump and store their milk. Parenting support groups and father mentorship programs are available at some companies. Take-home meals from company cafeterias are offered to ease time pressures, new parent information packages are distributed, and adoption assistance is provided. Some companies organize summer camps. In some organizations, pregnant employees are given reserved parking places, close to the company entrance. Other companies distribute family-oriented newsletters, provide overtime child care assistance, design tutoring programs, and develop on-site schools. If your company culture promotes family-friendly policies, numerous creative approaches could be designed to target the specific needs of the organization.

There are many child care options to consider. How should companies decide which options are right for them? The next chapter will answer that question.

NOTES

1. Milton Moskowitz and Carol Townsend, "100 Best Companies for Working Mothers," *Working Mother* (October 1993), 31.

2. Personal conversation with Tom Grubisich, October 1993.

3. United States Department of Education, *National Study of Before and After School Programs* (Portsmouth, NH: Research Corporation, 1993), 4.

4. Moskowitz and Townsend, "100 Best Companies," 60–61.

5. One source for activity kits is the Activities Club, P.O. Box 9104, Waltham, MA 02254-9104. (800) 873-5487.

6. *Wall Street Journal,* January 19, 1993.

7. The Conference Board, *Work-Family Roundtable: Flexibility,* vol. 1, no. 1 (December 1991).

8. Focus groups conducted for nationwide businesses in 1993 by Fried & Sher, Inc.

9. Moskowitz and Townsend, "100 Best Companies," 50.

10. Personal correspondence with Jeffrey Hough, September 1993.

11. Moskowitz and Townsend, "100 Best Companies," 50.

Chapter Three

■ ■ ■ ■ ■

Decisions: "You Can Sleep on a Matter Before You Decide, Unless You Have a Competitor Who Doesn't Need the Sleep"

A decision about child care is not easy. A child care benefit should help solve a problem, either an existing problem or an expected problem, and the price for the solution should be considered in light of the cost of the original problem. The question "Should we consider child care?" must be restated as "Should we consider a child care benefit, and, if so, which benefit will work best in our situation?" From the employees' point of view, there are four potential child care problems that affect their life at work.

First, child care may not be available to employees. Child care is difficult to find outside the hours of 7:00 A.M. to 6:00 P.M., Monday to Friday. It is also difficult to find care for children under age two and a half and for older children before and after school. Second, quality care may not be affordable to employees. Third, child care programs may not be readily accessible. Many parents must commute to child care and then head in the opposite direction to get to work, resulting in a longer commute. Such arrangements can add as much as two hours of commuting time daily. In addition, parents usually cannot transport school-age children to after-school programs.

The fourth problem concerns overall quality. Parents often agonize over child care situations, aware that their children are not receiving good care but unable to find or afford better child care. Another aspect of the quality issue is dependability. It is not uncommon for a parent to knock on the door in the morning and learn that a sitter is not working that day, or to be told on a Friday that that is the sitter's last day.

These are the problems that employees contend with. From the employers' point of view, these problems are often translated into company problems of absenteeism, tardiness, turnover, low morale, and decreased productivity. A child care decision should be targeted to the following two goals: easing the specific *company* problems that are attributed to child care issues, such as retention and productivity, and easing the most glaring child care problems of the *employees,* such as affordability and quality.

HOW DO WE DO A NEEDS ASSESSMENT?

You will need to conduct a comprehensive needs assessment consisting of four parts:

1. Examine your company's goals and corporate culture and look at any problems, such as tardiness or turnover, from the company's point of view.
2. Assess the employees' needs through focus groups and a needs assessment survey.
3. Perform a market study of available local child care.
4. Compare the data you have gathered with the child care options that are possible for your company.

You might want to consider hiring a child care consultant to help with the needs assessment process.

Corporate Needs Assessment

Start by attempting to determine existing problems that may be a result of employees' child care problems. Is tardiness or absenteeism a problem? How about employee turnover or employee recruitment? On days that schools are closed, are children at work disrupting productivity? If these problems exist, do they exist within all departments or only in selected departments? Include in this corporate needs assessment an analysis of what child care benefits your competitors are providing. Also, try to think ahead. Will predicted demographic trends in your area be likely to lessen or add to corporate child care problems in the future?

Next, assess the attitudes of management at all levels within the organization. Are your managers likely to support the study of child care issues and the potential provision of child care benefits? Is there a "champion" for this cause—someone who wants to take a leadership role? At Fannie Mae, for example, a female vice president who had the respect of other senior management was a forceful champion of an on-site emergency back-up child care center and took a businesslike, no-nonsense point of view to the decision-making process.[1]

Employee Needs Assessment

In conducting an employee needs assessment, first obtain qualitative information through focus group interviews. Properly conducted focus groups will pinpoint specific child care problems experienced by employees, highlight ways in which employee child care problems translate into corporate problems, help assess employee satisfaction with existing work-family programs, and provide valuable data and insight for the design of an effective quantitative employee assessment tool.

A focus group is a discussion, lasting one and a half to two hours, with a maximum of 12 employees grouped homogeneously (*e.g.*, night shift workers, mid-level managers). The small group encourages participation and allows for in-depth discussion of issues, and homogeneity encourages openness in the discussion. The employees' comments are strictly confidential. The employer and the focus group facilitator decide ahead of time the important topics to be covered in the discussion. The questions posed are open-ended and discourage griping. It is important that the facilitator emphasize that no commitments are being made to employees concerning future plans of the company.

The qualitative information gained from focus groups is used to help formulate an employee survey questionnaire, which will result in quantitative data. Properly designed and administered surveys can provide accurate statistical estimates within known levels of statistical reliability. Employee survey questionnaires are essential for understanding the true needs of the employee population as a whole. They help guard against the implementation of child care benefits that address the needs of a small vocal minority at the expense of the corporation or of larger but less vocal groups. Survey questionnaires also give numeric support to issues identified in focus groups and provide input for a cost-benefit analysis of various child care options the company is considering.

Because it is so important to gather proper information, let's take an in-depth look at the development of an employee survey tool.

Designing the Needs Assessment Survey. An effective employee child care needs assessment will be based on the issues and qualitative data gathered through the focus groups and on the understanding that child care needs are very diverse and segmented. A needs assessment will also take into consideration and reduce various response and nonresponse biases that might enter into the collection of data.

Employee child care needs vary greatly. Ages of the children and the number of children within families affect child care needs. Needs vary as to whether part-time, full-time, or periodic (holidays only, sick days only) care is desired. Working patterns of parents, differences in income, differences in family and household composition (such as a live-in grandmother), and differences in family values also affect child care needs. The needs of one-parent households are different than the needs of two-parent households. Child care needs also vary based on whether care is desired near the home or near the workplace. Differences in child care availability in the marketplace also have an impact on child care needs.

Assessing the range in employee child care needs is one of the most difficult, yet one of the most important, issues to address in a needs survey. Those designing child care needs assessments should include questions that address the variety of needs. The analysis of the needs assessment data should be designed so that the numbers of employees with similar needs can be identified.

Reducing Bias. For many years professional researchers have studied the causes and impacts of survey response biases. Three types of response bias[2] that may potentially impact the quality of data in child care needs assessments are social desirability biases, desire-to-please biases, and expectation-of-gain biases.

Social desirability biases arise when respondents do not answer questions honestly for fear that their answers go against the mores of society and will be viewed negatively. Desire-to-please biases occur when respondents provide inaccurate or distorted answers because they mistakenly believe that such answers are what researchers really want to hear. Expectation-of-gain biases occur when respondents believe that a particular pattern of responses will help to produce the end result they desire, even though the actual responses may be inaccurate or misleading.

The following steps can be taken to reduce response biases:

- Make it clear to survey respondents that the data collected in the needs assessment study will be kept completely confidential.
- Introduce the study as one that is designed to gather exploratory data, and explain that no decisions, pro or con, have been made to provide any child care benefits.
- Inform respondents that you are attempting to gather information that is as accurate and honest as possible.
- Consider alternative ways of asking specific questions to reduce potential response biases.

Ensuring a High Response Rate. Whether you attempt a census of the entire population or select a sample of the total population for your needs assessment, it is crucial that you obtain as high a response rate as possible from those who are surveyed. Low response rates can seriously damage the quality of survey results if those people who respond are unlike those people who do not. Nonresponse may be especially troublesome in a child care needs assessment because those with a need for child care, or those with a need for just one type of child care service, may be more likely to respond than others.

Surveys can be either self-administered or interview-administered. The Market Research Association has found that the average mail questionnaire gets a 15 percent to 30 percent response rate, while the average telephone survey gets a 60 percent to 65 percent response rate. It is possible, however, to do much better than that. The Office of Personnel Management requires a 70 percent return rate from its contractors. Telephone research firms often call home and work until they reach the targeted employee. The highest return rate we have achieved is 84 percent in surveying a 4,400-employee company spread among eight locations nationwide. Here are some tips for achieving a high response rate:

- Publicize, publicize, publicize! At least 10 days before the actual survey distribution date, begin posting flyers announcing that the survey is coming. Follow up every few days with either a newsletter announcement, a letter from upper management, voice-mail messages, or announcements at staff meetings. Build the anticipation.
- Organize the distribution well. Know how many surveys are being distributed to each department and shift. Establish a senior point of responsibility within each department. As needed, the senior point of responsibility should establish designated individuals within the department to

distribute and collect a percentage of the surveys. A drop-box return or a return through inter-office mail generally does not produce a high survey return.

- For nonexempt employees, it often works well to have someone from their peer group collect the surveys. Respondents can remain anonymous by placing surveys into a box or large envelope that their peer is passing around or holding.
- Establish a designated time within departments or shifts to complete the survey. The survey should only take about 15 minutes to complete.
- Know who is on vacation or out on leave when the survey is distributed and ask their peers to be responsible for getting them to complete the survey upon their return to work.
- Some healthy interdepartmental competition, with prizes or incentives for the highest return rates, often spurs enthusiasm and high responses.

Sampling is a valid method of research for companies with more than 1,000 employees. More reliable data will be gathered by surveying a smaller sample with a method that assures a high response rate than by surveying the entire population and getting a low response rate. If a probability sample is mathematically determined, the results can be interpolated for the whole population.

Asking the Right Questions. A survey instrument must be designed to gather two types of information—factual data and attitudinal information. Surveys can provide much necessary factual data, such as the total number of parents in the employee population, the number of single parents, and the number of children by age. Survey data can be used to create a profile of child care practices currently in use for each age group. Ask respondents the number of infants, toddlers, two-year-olds, three- to five-year-olds, and school-age children who are cared for by a spouse, a relative, a child care center, a caregiver in an employee's own home, a caregiver in another home, or a school-based program, and the number of children left on their own. Information for each of these categories and age groups must include whether the care is full-time or part-time. Factual data should also include the amount employees are currently paying for each of these types of care, the number of times employees have had to change their child care arrangements during the past year, the total family income by level, and the zip codes of employees' residences.

Attitudinal data that must be gathered includes employees' level of satisfaction with their current child care arrangements and what employees see as their most pressing problems in terms of finding, affording, or being satisfied with the quality of child care for each specific age group. Data should also indicate which of the following issues have impacted employees' work: finding emergency child care when regular arrangements fall through; finding care for a sick child; finding care during working hours; finding care for school-age children on school holidays, snow days, and the summer; finding care in a convenient location; needing more flexibility at work to accommodate special situations; and worrying about a child at home alone. Other attitudinal data should include employees' assessment of how much work they have missed due to child care problems and which specific child care options would benefit them the most. If the company is willing to develop a child care center should the need be shown, a direct question may be asked as to whether or not employees would plan to enroll their children.

Many companies are now doing comprehensive work-family surveys rather than just child care surveys. Questions concerning care problems with elderly parents and relatives as well as family members with special needs are included. Questions about flexible schedules and personnel policies may also yield helpful information.

It is equally important to ask a question which speaks to the equity issue. For example, "Do you support the idea of GO Systems implementing new programs to assist employees in better balancing their work and family lives even if you do not directly benefit from them?" Surprisingly, there is often tremendous support for these programs from employees who do not personally have work-family problems; coworkers' problems can affect the work of other members of the team. And, people really do care what happens to children.

The resultant survey data must be analyzed critically for short-term and long-term implications. Also, the data should be looked at as an indicator of the greatest employee needs. For example, suppose you are thinking about developing an on-site child care center. If the survey data indicate that there are many children who are four years old and up but few infants and toddlers, you may want to think about a school-age program rather than a program for infants through age 5, because not many employees would use a program for very young children in the next several years. In addition, you should plan for only about 50 percent of the number of spaces that respondents indicate they would use. This will be discussed further in the next chapter. Also, if you are thinking about instituting a discount or vendor program in several child care centers around town, and you have hundreds of employees who indicate that they need financial assistance to pay for their child care, it is possible that your employees may "use up" many of the spaces in those centers. What would be the public relations consequences for your company?

Analyzing the Child Care Market. The third step of the needs assessment process is conducting an analysis of the local child care market. Local resource and referral agencies can provide data about local child care programs and gaps in services in the community. You need to determine the number of existing child care services that are available to your employees by the types of child care need identified in your employee needs assessment. Identify key child care people in the community and interview them to get their perspective. They can share very helpful information about the community if you make an effort to listen and respond to any concerns that they may have. Contact several child care organizations to determine the type and quality of child care that they offer and the amount of space that they have available during your work hours. Also, contact local government agencies and school systems to learn what types of public child care programs are offered and what, if any, restrictions apply.

Evaluating Your Options. If you have successfully completed the three steps already mentioned, you will be in a very good position to evaluate the pros and cons of various child care options available to your organization. You can conduct a cost-benefit analysis to determine whether your organization can and should develop child care services, more flexible personnel policies, financial support programs, and/or informational services.

The decision of whether to offer a child care benefit, like other corporate decisions, should be based on hard facts. Consider these questions:

- What are the company's current or anticipated problems?
- Could they be related to child care?
- What hard data are on file already (such as ages of employees, sex, salary ranges by age and sex, zip codes of employees' residences, number of dependents)?
- What do we think the work force will look like five years from now?
- What hard data were gathered from the survey?
- What issues were raised in focus groups?
- What is available and what are the shortages in the local child care market?

- Which child care option will best meet the needs of the employees and the business goals of the company?
- Which child care options reflect the culture of the organization?

E-Mail>

17 August 1993. 16:26:08.44

From: Bob Roman

To: Sharon Klein; Sam Anderson

Subj: Child Care

Sharon, Sam, your report on options and needs assessment is excellent! I never imagined we'd have all these options. But I'm sure we can put together a good survey. The next step, I think, for a comprehensive report for George is to delve into some of the child care issues. Let's meet Monday at 2:00 to brainstorm.

NOTES

1.   Personal interview with Eugene Ritzenthaler, director of employee benefits, Fannie Mae, June 9, 1993.

2.   Many of the concepts expressed here concerning bias and sampling stem from the work of Gary Brown, executive vice president, Decision Data of McLean, Virginia.

Chapter
Four

■ ■ ■ ■ ■

A Child Care Center! What Are We Getting Into?

"Sharon, Sam, come in and sit down. It sounds like we're really moving forward with our information gathering. I think we might be able to sell the survey idea. We need to get the factual information on the employees and then consider what to do. I want to read you this short memo that George shot to me this morning.

Bob, I'm glad you gave me a quick update on the child care thing at the company picnic yesterday. I've been doing some thinking. If we go ahead with anything, I want absolute proof that the employees need it. I want excellent, accurate figures on cost—you might want to confer with Elinor. And remember, I want guarantees that anything we do will be absolute top quality, so don't give me any numbers that refer to a mediocre program.

"Enough said? O.K. Let's talk about other areas that we need to research."

Many companies are deciding that a child care center is the correct option for them, and because this decision involves many complicated issues, we will concentrate in the next few chapters on child care center development issues. This information is relevant to the development of any kind of center—on-site, near-site, consortium, emergency back-up child care, sick-child care, school-age child care, infant and toddler care, or preschool care.

An employer-supported child care center is an excellent option for some businesses to implement. How do corporate executives come to this conclusion? How many employees should a company have to consider opening a child care center? How many employees must express interest in order to warrant a child care center? These are the types of questions that are frequently asked. The answers, of course, are not simple and depend on several variables.

Is the employer expecting the child care center to be financially self-sufficient, or is the employer planning to subsidize ongoing operations? Is the employee population predominantly young or predominantly female? How far is the company located from where most employees live? Is it feasible to commute with children? Will the center care for children under age two? Will the center provide emergency or sick-child care? Does the employer want a child care center only for employees, or will it be open to the public? Is a consortium with other nearby employers possible? These questions all need to be answered before the employer can decide whether the need for child care is large enough to warrant the development of a child care center.

IS THE NEED FOR CHILD CARE GREAT ENOUGH?

There are some quick rules of thumb a company can use to determine whether a child care center is feasible. If a center enrolls infants to five-year-olds, around 80 children (or full-time equivalents for a part-time program) are needed for financial viability, *if* about 70 percent of those children are over age two. It is important to consider the ages of the children to be served when evaluating financial viability. Since one adult can care for fewer children under the age of two than four- or five-year-olds, these very young children are more expensive to care for because they require more staff. The true cost of caring for infants and toddlers is usually much more than parents can pay. Usually child care centers charge less than the full cost for infants and toddlers and more than cost for two- to five-year-olds to balance the budget; therefore, a center that does not enroll infants and toddlers needs fewer children to reach financial viability. It is important to note, however, that one of the greatest needs for child care throughout the country is infant and toddler care; if a new center decides not to take these very young children, it may be jeopardizing enrollment as parents look for centers that will take their babies. Also, please note that the market rate for a quality child care program may not be affordable for lower-level employees. We will discuss subsidized fees in detail in chapter 6.

Now you know that you need a minimum of 80 children if you want a financially self-sufficient child care center. How do you know whether you will have at least 80 children? Perform a needs survey with at least a 70 percent return rate. Look at the number of children who will enroll based on their parents' noted interest on the survey, and then assume that 50 percent of those children will not enroll for various reasons (grandma moved in, the woman down the street is wonderful, a sister-in-law is running a child care center close by, etc.). It is also important to look at the spread of ages in the survey responses. If most of the potential children are school-age, you need to think about a school-age program, not a preschool program. If the survey indicates a large amount of interest in child care for infants and toddlers, a center for infants through five-year-olds will probably work. The infants and toddlers will grow into the two-year-old and preschooler (three- to five-year-olds) spaces.

Another quick rule of thumb is that generally 2 percent to 3 percent of an employee population in a large, diverse work force can be expected to use a company-sponsored child care center at any one time. If 50 percent of your stated attendees coincides with 2 to 3 percent of your work force, you have a good number to plan with. If 50 percent of your stated attendees is higher than 2 to 3 percent of the total employee population, it may mean that you have a younger work force than average, or that child care programs are sparse in your area, and you may want to plan for more spaces than 50 percent of the stated attendees. If 50 percent is less than 2 to 3 percent, you may have a smaller number of employees who would use a child care center, and it might not be the best option for you. If the number of slots is close to 80, the center should work. If you come up with less than 80 slots, and you still want a center, you know that an ongoing subsidy will be needed since there will be fewer children to cover the overhead costs. If the number is much more than 80, that works, too. Larger centers are generally more financially stable. If you are thinking about a large center, please look carefully at chapter 7. Large centers need special consideration in the design phase.

Please also note that we are not *advocating* that a child care center be required to sink or swim on its own, without ongoing financial assistance. The question at this point is simply whether the employee need is great enough to warrant an on-site or near-site child care center. After estimating the number of children who will be enrolled, base your decision about whether to go ahead with a child care center or to explore other options on the reasons the company thinks a child care center would be a good idea (such as good public relations or decreased turnover) and the amount, if any, that the company is willing to subsidize the center on an ongoing basis.

If your needs survey does not show evidence that a full-time child care center for only your employees is the best option, you may still want to consider forming a consortium with other neighboring businesses, opening your center to community residents, or developing an emergency back-up child care center. Keep in mind that a back-up center must meet all the licensing criteria that a full-service center must meet, even though the back-up center may be quite small; a cost-benefit analysis is relatively easy to compute for such a service.

HOW LARGE ARE SUBSIDIES FOR CHILD CARE CENTERS?

Many companies subsidize the yearly operating costs of their centers from one-third to one-half of the budget, so that tuition fees are affordable for their employees and quality remains high. Child care is the fourth largest item in many family budgets—after taxes, housing, and food—with costs for care ranging from 7 percent to 25 percent of family income. Lower-income families pay a disproportionately higher percentage for child care, often as much as they pay for housing.

A recent report from Catalyst, *Child Care in Corporate America: Quality Indicators and Model Programs*,[1] stated that the average subsidy amount among centers that reported the information was 39 percent. Companies provide financial support in terms of starting the center (the average at 23 centers reporting to Catalyst was $503,415), operating the center (the annual average at 20 centers was $282,210), providing subsidies and scholarships for parents, and supporting the center through company resources, such as building and grounds and maintenance. According to the Catalyst report, "quality care requires an investment from the corporate sponsor."

On the other hand, child care centers sponsored by federal government agencies are expected to pay for their own ongoing operating costs, with the exception of space costs (under the Trible Amendment). Authorized in 1986, the Trible Amendment allows for the expenditure of public funds to provide space for child care facilities. These centers are, indeed, financially self-sufficient, but their tuitions are often too high for lower-level employees to afford. This is a major problem for federally supported agencies. Some centers try to solve the problem by undertaking large fund-raising projects to provide scholarship money to lower-level workers. A full discussion of center costs will take place in chapter 6.

WHAT IS QUALITY CHILD CARE?

Let's assume that after looking at company demographics and the results of your needs assessment, you believe the company as a whole and your employees would greatly benefit from a company-sponsored child care center. You are willing to look at the budgets involved and the cost to the company. But what about quality? George Oliver insists that when his name is on something, it is done the right way. Your company probably feels the same way. An employer-sponsored child care center is a reflection of the employer, and most companies understand that. So what is the right way? What is quality? And why is it so expensive to care for little kids?

It is interesting that we know more about quality when it concerns our clothing or furniture than we do about quality child care. We know to look at the kind of fabric our suits are made of and whether the tailoring is finished properly. We know the difference between solid wood furniture and veneered particleboard. With approximately 9,000,000 children in child care today,[2] we must also know about the quality care they require.

The quality of a child care center is a function of each tiny interaction between an adult and a child that occurs throughout the day. The ways adults challenge children to learn and grow emotionally, physically, socially, and intellectually; the manner in which adults speak with children; the love and patience that adults display with children; the understanding shown for each child's interests and fears—these are all indicators of quality. These concepts may seem somewhat nebulous when you are trying to plan for a center with hard dollars and bricks and mortar, but there are concrete ways to plan for such an end result.

NAEYC, the National Association for the Education of Young Children, has developed very specific guidelines for a quality program (for ordering information, see appendix G). These guidelines were developed for the NAEYC accreditation program, and they should be followed by all child care programs.

Quality depends on

- Child/staff ratios
- Group size
- Educational level of staff
- Staff salaries

- Ongoing training programs
- A well-educated and experienced director
- Ample toys, equipment, and supplies
- A safe, clean environment that promotes proper hygienic practices
- An open-door policy for parents

Child/Staff Ratios

Child care is a very staff-intensive business. Most of the costs are staff costs. A major indicator of quality is the number of children each staff person is responsible for. One staff person should care for only three babies. Four is stretching the limit. One staff person should care for only four toddlers, five or six two-year-olds, or eight or nine preschoolers (three- to five-year-olds).

Group Size

Another indicator of quality is group size. NAEYC recommends 6 to 8 infants, 6 to 12 toddlers, 8 to 14 two- and three-year-olds, and 16 to 20 three- and four-year-olds.[3]

Staff

The background and education of the staff is also a major indicator of quality. Teachers should have four-year degrees in early childhood education or a related field. Obviously, the more experience, the better. Assistant teachers should have a minimum of a high school degree with early childhood development classes and experience. Many assistant teachers have associate degrees in early childhood education from community colleges; many others have B.A. or B.S. degrees. All staff are role models for children; the children do not necessarily know who are teachers and who are assistants. The staff should also be culturally diverse. Children look to all adults for learning, comforting, and caring; therefore, all adults must be energetic, intelligent, nurturing, and caring people. There is no place in a quality center for minimum-wage part-timers who sit around until a supervisor tells them to do a specific task.

Staff Salaries

Another indicator of quality is staff salaries. How much are the teachers and assistants paid? They should be paid as close to public-school salaries as possible. Because of the great cost of salaries, this goal is hardly ever reached, but salaries of a corporate-sponsored center should be among the highest in town. With the best salary and benefits package, you can attract the best-quality employees and you will be able to reduce staff turnover. High staff turnover is the most accurate indication of poor quality. Children must have consistency in their caregivers, and you must do everything possible to retain your good staff people.

Ongoing Training

Ongoing training is another necessity in a quality child care center. The budget should include money for workshops, conferences, and ongoing in-service training. A commitment to ongoing education for the staff is as important as the commitment to ongoing learning for the children. Many centers try to reimburse a percentage of the costs of college or graduate school classes that are relevant to early childhood education. Some centers pay for membership in NAEYC for all staff.

Director

The director of the center is a major key to quality. He or she should be well educated (a master's degree is preferred) and should have a thorough knowledge of early childhood education as well as training in business operations, supervision of employees, public relations, marketing, and interpersonal relationships. From this list of necessary skills, you should realize that a terrific director is hard to find! When you do find your gem, the salary level needs to be commensurate with the demands of the job. You do not want your wonderful director leaving because she or he cannot afford to live with your salary and benefits package.

Toys, Equipment, and Supplies

Abundant supplies are essential. Because children learn from their play, they must have a variety of equipment, toys, and materials to play with, and everything must be appropriate to the various developmental levels of the children. For example, large, brightly colored foam blocks are good for toddlers, and hard wooden blocks are good for three- and four-year-olds. There must be enough duplicates of popular materials so that all the children have a chance to use them on a regular basis. You would not be happy sharing your best pen with seven other people each day, would you? Chapter 6 includes information on equipment costs.

Environment

Child care center design is an important ingredient of quality. Safety must be of paramount concern. In addition, the environment must be conducive to healthy practices. For example, there must be an adequate number of sinks near toilets, near diaper-changing tables, and in kitchens. Food-serving areas must not be close to bathroom areas or diapering areas. Safety factors associated with design will be discussed in chapter 7.

Open-Door Policy

A final indicator of quality is that parents can stop in for a visit with their children whenever they wish. Parents often enjoy having lunch with their children or volunteering in a classroom. Nursing mothers find an on-site child care center a godsend. You may run into a child care provider who says that parent visits are disruptive and upset the children. Nonsense! Children quickly get used to parents coming and going. If an individual child is going through a difficult stage of separating from mom or dad, the teacher or director may want to work something out with that parent, but these problems are not earth-shaking. The important thing is that parents have free access to the child care center. This is a quality-control mechanism: with a number of people going in and out of the child care center each day, there are many eyes watching what goes on. In our experience, parents have not abused the employer's expectations and do not spend inordinate amounts of time at the center.

WHAT GOES INTO A FEASIBILITY STUDY?

Now let's assume that you have completed your needs assessment and the results of your analysis indicate that you need a 100-child center. You understand the quality issues involved and are committed to doing things the right way. Before you can make an informed decision about whether to go ahead with the development of a child care center, you need to gather much more information. It is time to do a feasibility study. If you did not hire a child care consultant to work with you on the needs assessment—which would have been a good idea—you probably need some child care expertise at this point. Your feasibility study should include an analysis of all parts of the needs survey, including employee survey results, market study results, and focus group results, as well as a review of employee demographics and management's assessment of current problems such as absenteeism, tardiness, and turnover. The feasibility study should also include possible sites for child care centers; projected budgets and start-up, operating, and month-by-month cost projections for three years; risk factors; options for organizational structure, such as contracting out management or establishing a nonprofit corporation with employees as board members; and a description of the scope of the project with a time line for development if a decision is made to go ahead. Of course, this kind of information is needed whether you want to pursue the development of a full-service child care center, an emergency back-up center, a school-age program, or any other type of direct-service program. We will cover each of the topics of the feasibility study in the next few chapters.

Should you decide to hire a consultant to do a needs assessment or to produce a feasibility study, it is a good idea to write a request for proposals (RFP) and send the RFP to experienced and known consultants. You can find consultants through the NAEYC in Washington, DC; the Child Care Action Campaign in New York; the ACCCI: Society of Work-Family Professionals; and the National Work Family Alliance. (See appendix G for the addresses of these and other resource organizations.) You might also contact your state child care licensing organization or local Office for Children.[4] Your RFP should specifically request each of the types of information listed above and should require information about the consulting firm, the type of work it has done, resumes of its employees, client lists, a statement of its philosophy, and a list of references. It is important to try to find a consultant who is impartial, not one who is trying to sell services such as child care center management, resource and referral services, or financial aid plans. The consultant must always customize solutions to reflect the culture and goals of the client. The consultant is a diagnostician and creator of customized solutions.

To whom does the consultant report? Many companies appoint a task force of employees to work on the project. Often the task force reports to the vice president for human resources or to the work-family manager. On the task force sit representatives from all relevant parts of the organization, including facilities, finance, legal, and human resources representatives, along with union representatives if appropriate. It is important that the task force be comprised of high-level individuals who have access to appropriate information. The child care consultant reports to the chair of the task force. Sometimes the work-family manager works without an organized task force. In this case, the consultant reports to the work-family manager, and the work-family manager makes sure that the consultant receives the information needed to perform the feasibility study.

WHAT DOES DEVELOPING A CHILD CARE CENTER ENTAIL?

Here is a glimpse of part of your feasibility study: the scope of work for the development of a child care center. Yes, it is a big project!

Program Design

- Conduct needs assessment.
- Review results of needs assessment and employee demographics.
- Determine number and ages of children to be served.
- Determine size of groups, ratios, number of staff.
- Determine staffing pattern.
- Determine hours of operation.

Architecture

- Review site selected: roads, traffic circulation, parking, attributes, security, service access, noise, future expansion, outdoor play area.
- Develop space program design for space identification, requirements, and usage.
- Review schematic design of center with architect and ensure compliance with program requirements.
- Review construction documents for square footage, plumbing, and other specific child-related items.

Playground

- Determine playground design.
- Determine landscape plan for identification and removal of toxic plants, trees, and shrubs and new landscape installation.
- Secure contract for proper installation and maintenance of equipment.

Security

- Determine basic security needs.
- Investigate security systems and possible options (including tying into any preexisting systems).
- Finalize security system.

Financial Systems

- Order and install computerized systems.
- Secure federal ID number and set up federal tax withholding account.
- File for appropriate state withholding tax accounts.
- Prepare start-up and pro forma budgets.
- Prepare monthly projections from start-up to full enrollment.
- Set up banking system: signature cards, deposit tickets.
- Order disbursement system.
- Develop financial and bookkeeping procedures.
- Set up filing system.
- Set up payroll system.

Permits and Licensing

- Visit licensing office and collect all licensing forms.
- Request copy of fire safety standards from state fire marshal's office.
- Request copy of child care center regulations and any floor plan submittal instructions.
- Collect licensing forms from the Department of Human Services; the State Fire Commission or fire marshal; and the Department of Health, Office of Environmental Health Services, as deemed necessary.
- Submit floor plan to fire marshal according to guidelines.
- After construction, request county Health Department preopening inspection of facility if applicable.
- After construction, request fire safety inspection of facility.
- Ensure completion of required staff training and certification (such as child abuse prevention training, food handler training, TB tests, and medical examinations).
- Request facility evaluation from licensing specialist.
- Submit license application with attachments as required by state and local governments.

Founding Board/Steering Committee, If Applicable

- Hold meeting for employees interested in serving on board.
- Identify initial members for founding board.
- Conduct initial incorporators meeting.
- Determine philosophy and goals of center.
- Adopt the name of the corporation.
- Elect officers.

- Draft and approve articles of incorporation.
- File articles of incorporation with state.
- Draft and approve bylaws.
- Conduct orientation for board.

Board Calendar and Agenda Items

- Determine legal structure of operation.
- Write board manual.
- Set up board files.
- Apply for tax-exempt status.
- Establish committees (fund-raising, marketing, budget, etc.).
- Discuss board responsibilities.
- Discuss board and director roles.
- Approve budget and ensure adequate start-up funding.
- Prepare all business forms (employer ID number, payroll, withholding applications).
- Approve insurance coverage.
- Determine policies and procedures from which parent, staff, and curriculum handbooks are prepared.
- Arrange for annual meeting.
- Arrange for annual audit of finances.
- Develop and adopt quality control standards and measures using NAEYC guidelines.
- Plan fund-raising: develop philosophy, establish goals, identify events to be held, determine dates for events, plan for events, and ensure application has been made for license to solicit charitable funds.
- Write history of center.

Equipment and Supplies

- Prepare floor plan and room arrangements.
- Organize equipment order.
- Negotiate discounts.
- Prepare vendor lists.
- Order classroom, administrative, and kitchen supplies; furniture; playground equipment; and educational materials.
- Plan delivery schedule, with deliveries made over several days.
- Set up equipment and supply files.
- Develop inventory procedures.

- Discuss possible donations.
- Note which items will be depreciated and capitalized.

Insurance

- Determine required amounts of coverage.
- Procure insurance, including liability, property, workers compensation, umbrella, student accident, transportation, theft, and bonding insurance.
- Explore cost and availability of director and officers insurance.

Administration

- Draft handbooks.
- Prepare administrative forms.
- Review service contracts.
- Prepare recruitment plans for children and for staff.
- Develop files for administration, including forms for center administration, staff, children, and parents.
- Establish enrollment procedures.
- Organize and prepare enrollment packages.
- Plan for an enrollment orientation for parents and children.
- Make arrangements for janitorial and trash-collection services, define standards, and set housekeeping schedules.
- Develop structure for scholarship program.
- Investigate subsidies.
- Prepare scholarship materials.

Center Calendar

- Plan calendar for operation: staff training days, board meetings, staff meetings, holidays, special events, fund-raisers, parent conferences, professional conferences, health screenings, marketing events, staff evaluations.

Marketing

- Develop name and logo for center, fact sheet or brochure, stationery, etc.
- Develop general marketing plan.
- Design ads and business cards.
- Print brochures.

- Oversee installation of signs and outdoor lighting.
- Arrange for open houses, lunchtime seminars, coffees, and advertising via flyers and ads.
- Design and print flyers and posters to be distributed to potential clients.
- Inform local newspapers of opening dates and plans and contact other media.
- Arrange for informational meeting for parents.
- Develop an ongoing, long-range marketing plan.

Food Service

- Decide which meals will be provided.
- Determine how meals will be provided, stored, and transported.
- Plan menus to ensure a nutritious program that meets USDA requirements.
- Review kitchen requirements for meal service (check with Health Department).
- Identify and meet with potential caterers for meals.
- Identify bulk-food providers for snacks.
- Identify and meet with potential providers for paper products.
- Negotiate and sign contracts.
- Arrange for delivery schedules.
- File for USDA reimbursements (nonprofits and Title XX centers only).
- Prepare system for USDA data maintenance.

Staffing

- Write ads for director and staff.
- Advertise for director.
- Contact local Association for the Education of Young Children for candidates.
- Contact local child care agencies.
- Recruit staff (see chapter 8).
- Prepare interview questions for director and for staff.
- Interview director candidates, check references by telephone as well as in writing, conduct criminal record checks, and check education and experience for compliance with licensing regulations.
- Hire a director.
- Prepare director training plans and schedule.

- Interview staff candidates, check references, and conduct criminal record checks.
- Hire staff.
- Set up personnel records.
- Recruit volunteers, interns, and substitutes.
- Prepare volunteer, intern, and substitute handbooks.
- Send notification letters to applicants not hired.
- Prepare probation period guidelines and evaluation forms.

Staff Training

- Prepare staff information packets.
- Prepare staff orientation agenda.
- Arrange for curriculum training.
- Plan for staff orientation to include review of center philosophy, procedures, policies, handbooks, job descriptions, curriculum, behavior management, health and safety guidelines, and use of staff resource center.
- Arrange for staff to visit other centers and attend professional meetings.
- Develop guidelines for parent/teacher conferences and for staff meetings.
- Arrange for membership in NAEYC and other professional organizations.
- Order professional books, magazines, and newsletters.
- Have director plan and later arrange for professional development with each staff member.

Children and Curriculum

- Review curriculum model.
- Develop guidelines for preparing the environment.
- Prepare anti-bias, multicultural guidelines.
- Draft developmentally appropriate infant, toddler, twos, preschool, kindergarten, and school-age curriculum guidelines (based on NAEYC guidelines).
- Develop health and safety guidelines, outdoor play guidelines, and guidelines for effective discipline.
- Prepare planning forms for teachers.
- Set daily schedules.

Transportation

- Define transportation needs (such as transportation for field trips or school-age transportation).
- For school-age transportation, contact local school systems and determine school bus routes.
- Determine number and cost of field trips.
- Investigate purchasing or renting one or more mini–school buses.
- If a mini–school bus is rented or purchased, purchase necessary insurance, review driver regulations, and arrange for special driving permits (if required).

Parents

- Prepare plan for parent orientation.
- Arrange for parent education programs.
- Develop parent resource library.
- Create format for monthly newsletter and weekly memo for parents and board.
- Prepare and implement parent participation program.

Community

- Review potential relationships with local universities for interns, volunteers, staff resources, and classes.
- Develop relationships with appropriate community agencies, such as the local library.
- Note potential walking trips for field trips.
- Identify special services for children in the area.

Moving In

- Call all vendors to verify orders and delivery dates.
- Assemble inventory packages containing inventory procedures and copies of equipment lists by vendor and by room.
- Arrange for adequate manpower and equipment to unload trucks on delivery day.
- Keep a running count of all boxes as they are delivered and unloaded, and then check count against driver's count.

- Follow inventory procedures (separate boxes by age group, inventory each box before unpacking it, and cross-check contents against packing slip and original order).
- After equipment and supplies have been inventoried and any discrepancies noted, items can be unpacked, assembled, and placed in each area.
- After cold storage is hooked-up, arrange for delivery of any refrigerated or frozen goods.

Opening Week

- Establish weekly plan.
- Coordinate catered food arrangements.
- Develop staffing plan.

Grand Opening

- Determine date, time, and style of grand opening.
- Prepare guest list and invitations.
- Organize program and invite speakers.
- Arrange for refreshments, decorations, etc.
- Contact public relations department.
- Arrange for press coverage, if desired.

Development of a child care center generally takes nine months, but it can be done in as little as six months. One of our clients absolutely had to have an operating center in three months, and we accomplished the task, but it required a great deal of concentrated labor and little discussion on the client's end concerning alternatives. Try to plan for nine months. This time frame does not include building or renovation, but center development can take place simultaneously with building development. Construction from scratch usually takes 18 months.

Does it sound complicated? Here is the payoff:

> I'm thrilled to have a high quality child care center at my worksite, because I can keep in touch with my child and her teachers and verify to myself that everything is going well during the day. I am really recharged after lunch with my child because the quality at the center is so high my mind is totally at rest and I can concentrate 100 percent on my work.

This enthusiastic comment is from a mother of a child at Langley Children's Center, at the Central Intelligence Agency.

Here is the way Ben Cohen and Jerry Greenfield of Ben & Jerry's Homemade describe their experience:

> People—all working together, pulling together for the same thing—that's what our company is about. People's work lives are integrally related with their family lives; you can't separate them even if you try. . . . Having a center on-site meets the objectives of the parents in our company; if you meet the needs of the people who are working for you, you are meeting the objectives of the company. It sounds schmaltzy, but happy people make a happy company.[5]

Maria Elwood, the director of Arnold & Porter's emergency back-up child care center in Washington, DC, says, "We estimated the center saved $500,000 in attorney time in 1992 that would have been lost."[6]

Donna Baughman of the Putman Companies notes, "In addition to combating absenteeism and productivity problems, the availability of emergency child care at our company is positioning Putman as a work and family leader in the recruitment marketplace. People want to interview with Putman because of it."[7]

NOTES

1.   Catalyst, *Child Care in Corporate America: Quality Indicators and Model Programs* (New York: Catalyst, 1993), 8.

2.   Ellen Galinsky and Dana Friedman, *Education Before School: Investing in Quality Child Care* (New York: Scholastic Press, 1993), 39.

3.   National Association for the Education of Young Children, *Accreditation Criteria & Procedures of the National Academy of Early Childhood Programs* (Washington, DC: National Association for the Education of Young Children, 1984), 41.

4.   See appendix D, "Current Child Day Care Licensing Offices," for addresses and telephone numbers for these organizations.

5.   Bonnie Neugebauer, "From Cherries Garcia to Child Care—The Story of Ben & Jerry's Children's Center," *Exchange Magazine* (November/December 1990), 41.

6.   Carol Kleiman, "Day Care Dilemma," *Chicago Tribune,* March 1, 1993.

7.   Joy Cohan, "Back-up Child Care Targets Absenteeism, Productivity at the Putman Companies," *Personnel Journal* (October 1992), 3 (supplement).

Chapter Five

■ ■ ■ ■ ■

Legal Issues: "The Good of the People Is the Chief Law"

"Hi, Bob. Sharon."

"Good morning! How was your weekend?"

"Great, Bob. Listen, I think what we should propose to George on this child care thing is to do a feasibility study which would include the whole needs assessment procedure, as well as a thorough analysis of child care center issues such as facilities, finances, and legal issues. But for the report I think we need some basic knowledge of the issues involved. I'd like us, next, to run a memo to Larry Ficini with some background on what we're working on, and I'll see if I can meet with someone from his legal office."

"Well, you had a profitable weekend thinking about this! Sounds good, but let's meet at 1:00 today so you can brief me more on what you're thinking. George would probably like to see a plan in parts—do the needs assessment to determine whether there is sufficient need before we go ahead with a whole feasibility study. But you're right, we need as much background as possible. We'll do a quick update on where we are. I think we just need 15 or 20 minutes."

WHAT LEGAL STRUCTURES ARE POSSIBLE FOR A CHILD CARE CENTER?

A child care center supported by a corporation can be structured legally in a variety of ways. When you first think about a child care center, you may run into a quandary of sorts. On the one hand, you may want a child care center that meets the specific needs and reflects the corporate culture of your business so that you have control over policies and procedures. On the other hand, you probably have had your fill of horror stories about child abuse and lawsuits and are concerned about liability risks for your company. The legal structure of the child care center speaks to issues of control and liability, but it is a continuum. The more control you want over the center, the greater is your liability exposure. The more decisions you make regarding the center, the more you can be held liable for those decisions. We do not, however, subscribe to the thinking that a child care center is fraught with risk and liability. When a center is developed properly and managed well, the risk is not large. Risk management is discussed later in this chapter.

The child care center can be a department of your corporation. Many hospitals structure their child care centers in this way. In this case, child care center staff are employees of the supporting corporation and receive the same salaries and benefits as equivalent employees in other departments.

The child care center can be a wholly-owned subsidiary. There may be tax advantages to a corporation electing this option.

The center can be established as a separate nonprofit corporation, with employees sitting on the board of directors. The employee board members can be a cross-section representation of the corporation, parents of children enrolled, or a mix, perhaps even including representatives of the local community. This type of center often qualifies for 501c3 tax-exempt status with the IRS. Nonprofit structures are popular structures for child care centers and have their advantages. Since child care centers are always so tightly funded, any excess income should be plowed back into the program. Child care should not be thought of as a profit center for the corporation. Sometimes the child care center board of directors will run the center, with the center's director reporting directly to the board. Sometimes the board of directors will contract with a professional child care management firm or with a national child care center chain to run the center. Any of these groups would have to work with the board of directors of the nonprofit corporation. Decisions about who runs the daily operations of the center all have financial, liability, and quality implications.

A corporation can contract with an outside group to run the center without a board of directors. The group could be a management company, a national chain, or a local child care provider.

A corporation can join with other corporations to develop a consortium child care center. The center can be developed as a separate child care corporation with board-member representatives from each of the participating corporations. A center director who reports to the board could run operations, or the consortium can contract out for services as described above. The consortium model does not necessarily mean the least amount of corporate control over the center. The amount of corporate control depends on the composition of the board of directors as set forth in the by-laws.

CAN WE DISCUSS THE L-WORD?

We sure can! In this section we will talk about liability, risk management, insurance, child abuse, licensing, and security issues. Remember the quandary we talked about—the control-liability continuum? More than a continuum, the relationship between control and liability could also be represented by a Venn diagram with two overlapping concentric circles. Liability risk can be diminished by asserting some control over your child care center, particularly if the object of your control is to maintain high quality. If you insist on child/staff ratios and group sizes that meet the National Association for the Education of Young Children (NAEYC) national accreditation standards, education and training levels for staff that ensure professionalism, salaries that are high enough to attract and retain good people, an on-site director with the skills and experience to do the job right, and a safe, clean facility, then you will have gone a long way toward reducing liability risks. On the other hand, if you decide to take an arm's length approach and contract out all responsibilities, it would be up to the courts to decide whether your company could be held liable in a lawsuit. They may decide that you are not liable; however, you will have done nothing to prevent the occurrence of a lawsuit in the first place. Needless to say, a lawsuit can mean some negative press for your company.

If you pursue options other than a child care center, you must also be aware of liability issues. Whether you are purchasing slots in a community center, collaborating with another organization for a school-age program, or developing a network of family child care homes, you must insist that any program you are associated with meets high standards. Liability risk is also influenced by the amount of parental choice involved. For example, in a voucher program, employees can usually use any legal type of child care they select, while in a vendor program the company may choose two or three sites to negotiate discounts. If the company preselects eligible child care for the parent, this might be interpreted as evidence that the company accepted some liability for the program.

Some reassurance is warranted here, however. Although it has been very difficult for analysts to gather appropriate data on claims, it appears that the number of lawsuits against child care centers is very small. A December 1989 publication from the U.S. Department of Labor entitled *Employer Centers and Child Care Liability Insurance* is a comprehensive examination of this subject. The summary of claims data in this publication states, "Analysis of a small number of claims shows that many of those losses might have been controlled, had providers taken adequate steps to reduce risk. . . . claims average less than $1000." The report also notes, "Respondents to the *Federal Register* request [for information] report very little claims experience." A 1989 survey by *Child Care Information Exchange* magazine, as quoted in the Labor Department study, found that 78.4 percent of respondents reported having experienced no claims or litigation, even though they had been in business an average of 15 years. Of the 21.6 percent reporting claims, most were for minor medical expenses or accidents. According to a 1987 study by S. L. Hofferth and D. A. Phillips in *Work & Family Program Models and Policies*: "90% of child care providers have never had a claim filed against them, and of those who have, 80% report claims totaling less than $500." The consulting firm Human Services Risk Management of Austin, Texas, reported at a 1989 Bureau of National Affairs conference that it knew of no claims or awards against an employer-supported child care center.

WHAT ABOUT INSURANCE?

Any child care center must carry insurance. It is the first step in risk management. If the child care center is structured as part of the company, the company's insurance carrier may be willing to extend coverage to the child care program. If not, there are a variety of insurance carriers that will insure child care centers.[1] Child care centers should be covered by comprehensive general liability, excess liability, student accident, and workers compensation insurance.

Comprehensive general liability coverage includes coverage for bodily injury, damage to other people's property, and the cost of legal defense if the center is sued. The coverage must be in place even if the injury occurs away from the program site (such as on field trips, walks in the neighborhood, or trips to public playgrounds). Check carefully to see whether the liability package also includes contractual liability; personal injury insurance against claims of libel, slander, and invasion of privacy; owner's and tenant's liability; fire legal liability; property insurance; and product liability for food served. The same package, or additional insurance, must cover business personal property.

Excess liability coverage provides coverage over the top of the general liability coverage. Often child care centers buy a $1,000,000 basic liability package and supplement that with a $1,000,000 excess liability policy. Of course, the amount of insurance you buy is somewhat dependent on the size of the center. You should know that many states mandate minimum insurance coverage in their child care licensing regulations (more on that to come!), but the minimum amounts mandated may not be adequate. Student accident coverage pays medical bills of children injured at the center, usually on an excess basis to their personal health insurance.

In addition, child care centers may buy employee dishonesty coverage (bonding) for employees handling money, vehicle insurance for buses to transport children, non-owned and hired automobile insurance to protect the center when employees use their own cars for center business (such as going to the bank, post office, or supply store), and directors and officers insurance to cover board members' actions. It should be noted that some states limit the liability of directors of nonprofit organizations; the National Center for Nonprofit Boards in Washington, DC, has excellent material on this subject.[2]

IS CHILD ABUSE COVERED BY INSURANCE?

No criminal acts can be covered by insurance. However, child care centers need coverage for allegations of child abuse, which may well be proven false. Many insurance companies specifically exclude coverage for physical or sexual abuse. Some carriers do, however, cover allegations of abuse in limited form. It is very important to read each policy and discuss the coverage with your insurance agent so that you are aware of exactly what is and is not covered. It should be noted that child sexual abuse cases arising in child care centers account for only 1.5 percent of the total number of child sexual abuse cases.[3] In the section on risk management at the end of this chapter, we suggest several ways to minimize the risk of physical or sexual abuse.

WHAT IS LICENSING?

All states require that child care programs meet state licensing regulations. Some states exempt certain types of programs from licensing, such as hospital-based programs or programs sponsored by religious institutions. You must check your own state's regulations.[4] *Licensing regulations are not necessarily an adequate indicator of quality.* They represent a floor below which no center can legally operate. Licensing regulations usually address such issues as number of sinks and toilets, amount of square footage required per child, staff/child ratios, staff educational or training requirements, and sometimes discipline. Regulations vary widely from state to state. For example, in Maryland one adult can care for only three infants, but in South Carolina one adult can care for eight infants. Eight infants! In any case, you must check your state licensing regulations. Some counties and cities also have regulations that must be met. If it is not evident that there is a county or city Office for Children, your state licensing office can give you the appropriate local office. Regulatory offices may use the terms *registration, certification,* or *accreditation* in place of or in addition to *licensing.* Remember, simply meeting licensing requirements is not enough to ensure quality. As explained in chapter 4, excellent quality guidelines have been written by the NAEYC.

HOW CAN WE LESSEN THE RISK?

Sorry if we've scared you. We have been in the child care business for 25 years and have not had any major problems. The point we are trying to make is simply that forewarned is forearmed. There are many ways to minimize risk, and most are quite easy to implement. Risk management is important, regardless of the child care options you may consider. For example, if you decide to fund an existing child care center in the community to expand its services, be sure that the center meets quality standards and minimizes its liability risks.

Policies and procedures for operations must be carefully thought through and documented in writing so that staff and parents understand clearly what is expected of them, and what the center will and will not do. These policies and procedures are usually written in a parents' handbook and in a staff handbook. The staff handbook should clearly explain all personnel policies and procedures (such as time sheets, request for leave, and staff meeting requirements); center policies on discrimination, child abuse or neglect, and grievances; detailed standard operating procedures; and detailed job descriptions. The parents' handbook must detail admissions policies and procedures and operating policies and procedures. The more clearly things are spelled out, the less likely there will be misunderstandings and disgruntled staff or parents.

Another way to minimize the risk of lawsuits is less clear-cut but extremely important: all center personnel must adopt an attitude of cooperative understanding with parents. Teamwork must be fostered between parents and staff. Defensiveness on the part of staff is inappropriate and ineffective. In a conflict, the goal should be to work toward consensus on a plan of action. A win/win solution is always best.

Staff-hiring procedures must be thorough. Review resumes carefully; hold personal interviews; check transcripts; phone at least three references, including professional references; conduct criminal record checks, if possible; and require a doctor-signed physical examination form, which includes certification for required immunizations. Everything, including notes from interviews and reference checks, must be carefully documented and filed. State licensing regulations sometimes require certain information before hiring also.

Staff training is an important component of risk management. All staff and volunteers should be trained in how to prevent, identify, and report child abuse. Information on child abuse identification and reporting should be included in the staff handbook and in the child care resource center. Usually laws requiring reporting of suspected abuse are quite specific. Community resources are often available; contact your state or local Department of Social Services. Other types of important training include general training on communication skills and on appropriate discipline.

The physical design of the child care center and playground is critical. Proper design can go far toward lessening the risk of injury and abuse. Chapter 7 is dedicated to design issues.

The security of the children and the facility must be maintained. Only authorized people—parents, staff, and corporate liaisons—should have free admittance. Policies and procedures must require parents to name persons who may and who may not pick up their children. Staff must be diligent in only allowing a child to leave the center with someone authorized in writing by the child's parent (custodial parent, if appropriate). It is a good idea to require that photos of people other than parents who are authorized to pick up children be kept at the center so that staff can check to make sure a strange person is truly authorized. Parents must be allowed to come and go whenever they wish. This can be a true risk management tool, especially if parents are encouraged to come to the director whenever they question anything they see.

We must refer you back to chapter 4's section on quality. A well-run, high-quality child care center is not at great risk for serious accidents, abuse, or lawsuits.

RESOURCE ORGANIZATIONS

Child Care Law Center
22 Second Street, 5th Floor
San Francisco, CA 94105
(415) 495-5498

National Lawyer's Committee for Civil Rights under Law
1450 G Street, NW, Suite 400
Washington, DC 20005
(202) 662-8600

National Center for Nonprofit Boards
2000 L Street, NW, Suite 411
Washington, DC 20036
(202) 452-6262

Child Care Action Campaign
330 Seventh Avenue, 18th Floor
New York, NY 10001
(212) 239-0138

NOTES

1.   See appendix C, "Child Care Center Liability Insurance Carriers," for a list of insurance carriers.

2.   National Center for Nonprofit Boards, 2000 L Street, NW, Suite 411, Washington, DC 20036.

3.   N. R. Page, "The Insurance Crisis: Who's Looking After Day Care?" *Harvard Women's Law Journal* 9 (Spring 1986), 200, 203–05; House Select Committee on Children, Youth and Families, *Child Care: The Emerging Insurance Crisis: Hearings Before the House Select Committee on Children, Youth and Families,* 99th Cong., 1st sess., July 18, 1985 (part one) and July 30, 1985 (part two) (testimony of Thomas L. Birch, legislative counsel, National Child Abuse Coalition).

4.   See appendix D, "Current Child Day Care Licensing Offices," for a list of licensing offices.

Chapter Six

■ ■ ■ ■

Finances: Poetry, Philosophy, and the Bottom Line

"That was an incredible match, Elinor! I thought we were finished when I kept double faulting, but you were sure able to slip in a few aces!" Bob ran the wet towel over his forehead again as he and Elinor walked back toward the clubhouse.

"It was a great match! Thanks for asking me to join you. I needed a good game like that more than I realized. How about we sign up for the mixed doubles tournament?"

"Sure! That'd be great! Listen, I'm glad you feel indebted to me for a good game. After we change, I have a document I'd like you to look at. Remember the child care research my department's doing? My staff put together some numbers and I think it would be helpful if you'd look at the methodology they're using and see what you think."

"An ulterior motive, huh, Bob? If we play in the tournament, what kind of additional work will I find on my desk?" Elinor laughed.

I think no matter how we fudge it
Our true colors will appear in the budget

Let's talk poetry. Let's talk philosophy. This is what a budget is: poetry and philosophy. A budget is poetry because it has a definite rhythm and balance; one line item affects another. A budget is philosophy because it tells clearly and concisely what a company's underlying beliefs are. Are we willing to spend the money to pay adequate salaries to child care center staff? If we are, it is because we believe that it is essential to the children's development that we attract and retain well-educated and experienced staff. Are we willing to spend adequate funds to purchase the toys and equipment children need? If we are, it is because we believe that children need these things in order to develop properly and learn, and that the early years are very important. The budget eliminates flowery language and excuses; it is a clear numerical statement of what we consider important.

In this chapter we will discuss the start-up costs of developing a child care center, the costs of ongoing operations, budgeting for the start-up years, scholarships and issues of affordability, and fund-raising ideas. These costs are relevant to emergency back-up centers and school-age programs as well as full-service centers for infants through five-year-olds. Let's begin with the start-up costs.

WHAT'S THE BOTTOM LINE HERE?

There are several categories of start-up costs: the cost of construction, the cost of equipment and supplies, the cost of personnel prior to opening, and the cost of prepaid items. Construction costs for building a new building generally range from $80 to $150 per square foot, depending on local costs and design complications. As will be discussed in chapter 7, you should estimate 100 gross square feet per child. For example, if you are planning to construct a child care center for 100 children, you can estimate construction costs:

> 100 children x 100 square feet per child = 10,000 square feet needed

> 10,000 square feet needed x $100 square foot = $1,000,000 construction costs

Renovation costs range from $50 to $100 per square foot, depending upon the extent of the renovation needed. Because we advocate a semiopen space design, the construction is fairly simple. The greatest construction costs are for plumbing—many little children mean many little sinks and potties. Not included in these construction costs are the cost of any land, the cost of extensive site work, architectural and civil engineering costs, zoning costs, state and local fees, testing costs, utility hookups, and playground development. Larger buildings will yield more efficiencies in costs. The costs cited assume that the building will house children under two years old. There are more extensive building codes for children under two, so the center described here is more expensive than a center for older children would be.

The second category of start-up costs is equipment and supplies. You can plan for approximately $700 per child for infants, $450 per child for toddlers, $500 per child for two-year-olds, $375 per child for three- to five-year-olds, and $300 per child for kindergarten and elementary school-age children. For what, you say? For tables, chairs, cots, cribs, shelves, cabinets, toys, and equipment.

Next, consider personnel costs. Your child care center director and support staff should be brought on board several months before opening. Teaching staff should be brought in two weeks before opening for training, organizing, and meeting children and parents. You also need to budget for any outside expertise, such as a child care specialist, lawyer, or accountant. You may want a child care consultant or management firm to guide the project through from start to opening day.

A prepaid cost is usually insurance for the first year. This must be paid before opening and so becomes a start-up cost. Operating losses due to underenrollment are another start-up cost to consider. The amount of start-up losses depends upon the length of time it takes for center enrollment to reach the predetermined level, which in turn depends on the number and ages of children to be enrolled. Naturally, a smaller center takes less time to fill than a large center. It is not unusual for a 100-child center to take two years, or even a little longer, to fill. Usually the slots for the youngest children are filled first, and these children grow into the slots for three- to five-year-olds. School-age slots usually fill up quickly, too. The reason for this pattern is that there is a nationwide shortage of care for children under two and for school-age children, but parents have more child care choices available to them for three- to five-year-olds. The quality of the center also influences enrollment. Positive word of mouth from parents will be a tremendous help in filling the center quickly and cutting down on start-up operating losses. Another critical factor is the cost of care. Tuitions must be competitive with the rates of other local child care centers. Finally, start-up cost budgeting should include a contingency provision. A minimum of 2 percent is common.

WHAT GOES INTO A CHILD CARE CENTER BUDGET?

An operating budget for a child care center is like a poem. The problem with child care in this country, however, is that the style of the budget poem is closer to the style of Edgar Allen Poe than it is to that of, say, Ogden Nash, which would be much more appropriate for preschoolers. Gwen Morgan, professor at Wheelock College, first coined the term "trilemma" to refer to the budgeting problem of child care. A simple dilemma does not cover the issues involved! The three elements of the trilemma are personnel costs, tuition costs, and staff/child ratios. The largest part of the child care center expenditures (80 percent or more of the budget for a high-quality center without space costs) is personnel costs. Child care is a very staff-intensive business. Historically, child care center budgets were balanced because their staff accepted wages far below what their education, experience, and job description warranted. Low salaries were offered because parents could not afford to pay tuitions that would support appropriate salaries. At the same time, staff/child ratios are an important indicator of quality. The fewer number of children that each staff person must care for, the greater the quality of care each child can receive. The more staff people you have, however, the higher the personnel costs and the less affordable to parents the center becomes. So the trilemma has to do with quality and cost, which depend on the number of staff and the amount they are paid. The more staff and the more they are paid, the higher the potential for quality. But the more staff and the more they are paid, the less parents can afford the resulting tuitions. The number of staff, their salaries, and the resulting cost to parents form the trilemma. The trilemma can be broken when it is recognized that parents cannot pay the true cost of child care anymore than they can pay the cost of public school education or college. Other funding sources must kick in in addition to parent tuitions. This is beginning to happen in employer-sponsored child care.

The Department of Defense runs the largest employer-supported child care system in the country. The military has solved the trilemma problem for its parents. M. A. Lucas, chief of Army Child Development Services, states: "The Services have broken the link between compensation and fees. Parents now pay on a sliding fee scale according to total family income, and staff are paid based on their training and performance. The military makes up the difference between the cost of care and the parent fees. Since we instituted this policy, our child care staff turnover has been cut dramatically, and turnover is directly linked to quality."[1]

Other employers also have solved the trilemma by subsidizing the child care budget each year. The Committee for Economic Development found that most companies with on-site or near-site child care centers subsidize the centers substantially. Examples cited include Campbell Soup Company, which underwrites approximately 40 percent of its center's operating budget; Champion International, which subsidized its center by $175,000 in 1990; and SAS Institute, which provides subsidies to two centers. Andrew C. Sigler, the CEO of Champion International, considers the child care center extremely worthwhile. He has specifically noted that because the company has a child care center, it has been able to attract top-rate local people.[2]

What exactly goes into a child care center budget? First, we need to identify the required costs for a high-quality center (see Figure 6.1). Salaries and associated benefits are the largest chunk of the budget. In a center that does not pay space costs—and most employer-sponsored centers consider the space an in-kind contribution—a good 80 percent of the budget should go for salaries and benefits. This line item is a definite statement of philosophy. If you believe that a stable staff of well-educated and experi-

Figure 6.1
Sample Expenses of an Employer-Supported Child Care Center

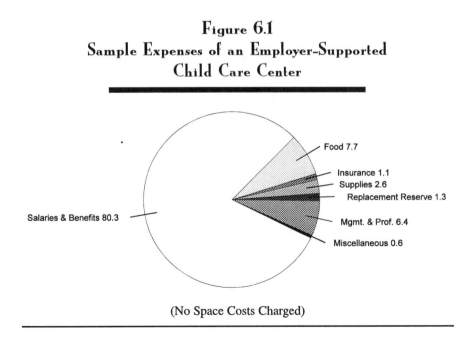

Food 7.7
Insurance 1.1
Supplies 2.6
Replacement Reserve 1.3
Salaries & Benefits 80.3
Mgmt. & Prof. 6.4
Miscellaneous 0.6

(No Space Costs Charged)

enced people is important for the proper development and learning of the children, then you will pay attractive salaries and benefits to attract and retain an excellent staff.

If your child care center is not being run as a department of your corporation, and child care center staff will not receive the same benefits as other employees, the following are traditional child care center staff benefits:

- Annual leave. (We recommend two weeks to start.)
- Sick or personal leave. (We recommend two weeks.)
- Health insurance. (The child care center should pick up 50 percent to 90 percent of the cost.)
- Life insurance. (This usually comes as a package with health insurance.)
- FICA, unemployment insurance, and workers compensation insurance.

The next largest expenditure item is food. Children need to be served snacks and lunch, and, depending on the hours of your center, breakfast and dinner. Children also need nutritious food. If most of their food intake occurs while they are at the child care center, it is essential to their development that they be served a balanced diet, free from too much sugar, salt, and additives. Chocolate cupcakes and sodas are not acceptable! If you are getting reimbursement from USDA (more on this soon), nutritional guidelines are clearly delineated.

The next expenditure item may be a fee for a professional management firm or a child care consultant. If you contract out to a vendor, they will want to budget in a profit or a fee for their services. If you have a small center, an experienced child care center director may be able to run the center by himself or herself, with perhaps some outside services depending upon his or her skills. In any case, whether you have carefully selected an experienced and successful director or hired a professional firm, you must be sure to operate your center with knowledgeable people at the helm.

The other expense items are relatively small. They include

- Staff development. Money must be budgeted for staff training, workshops, and conferences, and perhaps support for college courses. This item may be included in the benefits line.
- Employee relations. Morale building activities for staff, such as lunches, parties, and flowers for special occasions, are important. Many centers have a "sunshine fund," to which employees donate to celebrate one another's birthdays, but it is still important to have a little money budgeted for special events.

- Repairs and maintenance. The sponsoring corporation provides these items, but some money should be budgeted for emergencies.
- Office supplies.
- Curriculum supplies. Consumables that have to be replaced on an ongoing basis, such as paint, paper, and paste, need a budget line.
- Center supplies. Consumables such as plastic gloves, diaper-changing paper, and sponges are needed for hygienic reasons.
- Insurance. Insurance costs about $70 per child.
- Field trips. If the center will have to pay admission for any field trips that are planned for the children—to puppet shows, musical events, hayrides, or pumpkin picking—those costs must be budgeted.
- Professional fees. Some money should be budgeted for legal and accounting services. At a minimum, you will need a yearly audit.
- Transportation. This will be a small item if you only plan to rent a school bus a few times a year for special field trips, but it will be a large item if you own or lease a bus to transport children daily. In that case, you need to budget for lease costs or payments, gas, and upkeep.
- Advertising. You may not have to advertise in local media for children, but you will have to advertise for staff. Consider the cost of an employment ad in your local paper on a regular basis.
- Miscellaneous. This is a very small line that includes expenses for items that do not fit into other categories. We often use .02 percent of expenses.
- Contingency. We recommend 2 percent budgeted here for any other line items underestimated and for a margin of error.
- Replacement reserve. You must budget a percentage of the cost of your equipment to be set aside each year for use when equipment replacement is needed. Take the total cost of all your equipment and divide it by 8 (an 8-year life is generally accepted), and set aside that amount of money each year in the replacement reserve.
- Shortfall. A minimum 2 percent shortfall should be figured for tuition that is not collected because of time lapses in enrollment and bad debts.

Where does the money come from to cover these expenses? The center's income can come from several sources (see Figure 6.2). The first, usually the largest, source of income is tuition. Tuitions are determined once all the costs are identified. The total cost for each age category of children is divided by the number of children to be enrolled in each age category. This gives you the tuition amounts if each age category of children were to pay for itself. In practice, however, the tuitions for children under age two would

Figure 6.2
Sample Income of an Employer-Supported
Child Care Center

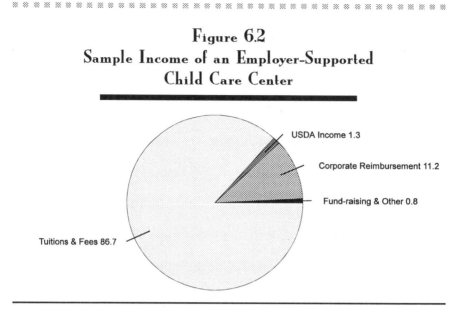

usually be too high to be affordable. As a result, the tuitions for the younger children are usually subsidized by the tuitions for the older children. You should look carefully at the market rates for child care in your locale. If your tuitions are quite a bit higher, your quality is probably going to be quite a bit higher, also. However, you may decide to subsidize the center in order to bring the rates down to the market rates. Figure 6.2 shows an 11.2 percent corporate reimbursement for this reason.

Another source of income is enrollment and application fees. The application fee is paid when an application is submitted and the child is placed on the waiting list. The enrollment fee is paid when the parent and child sit down with the center director and actually enroll in the program.

Fund-raising is another source of income. We believe, however, that the line item for fund-raising should be very small. As uncertain an item as fund-raising should not be relied upon to balance the operating budget. Fund-raising money can be used for a specific purpose not included in the operating budget. For example, fund-raising income might be used to fund scholarships for children from lower-income families or to buy a new major piece of equipment. Interest income on bank accounts and investments of reserve funds can also be planned on for income.

Another source of substantial income, if your child care center qualifies, is U.S. Department of Agriculture (USDA) partial reimbursement for food costs under the Child Care Food Program. Generally, private nonprofit child care corporations are eligible, but some other types of legal structures may qualify. USDA reimburses an amount for each child, depending on that child's family-income level. Three levels of reimbursement are mandated, but, for a general idea of reimbursement amount, consider this: in a 100-child center, the USDA reimbursement could bring the center a minimum of $10,000 per year.

These items comprise a very conservative budget, which is the proper way to budget. Income is minimized and expenses are maximized. There are pockets of budgeted expenses throughout the budget which may not be realized—shortfall, miscellaneous, and contingency expenses.

WHAT ABOUT THOSE START-UP LOSSES?

Right! We have discussed the start-up costs and the ongoing operational costs. One more budget is needed. You need to figure out your start-up operational losses to add to your start-up budget. The center will operate at a loss until you reach your enrollment goal.

You must first estimate the number of children who will start on opening day. The original enrollment depends to a large extent on the time of year you open. If you open in the beginning of September, you will have the best chance of optimizing your original enrollment, since many families arrange child care plans to coincide with the beginning of the school year. Mid-June is also a good time to open, especially if you start with a school-age program for the summer. January openings can also work well, because many families make child care plans to begin with the new year. Do not open in November or December if you can help it. People are too pre-occupied with the holidays to make new child care arrangements.

Another important factor in estimating starting enrollment is the amount of preopening publicity that the center will be given. If all employees know about the center in detail (philosophy, curriculum, hours, cost) and have several opportunities to meet the management, center director, and even the staff, opening enrollment will be higher than if no arrangements are made for preopening events.

You must think of enrollment in terms of the age groups of the children. The younger groups will probably fill up quickly, while the preschoolers may not fill up for a couple of years. This phenomenon is not good for operating losses, because the younger children generally do not pay their entire costs, while the preschoolers generate income in excess of expenditures. Notice the poetic balances here. Your poem will be off-meter until your center is fully enrolled.

Break down your monthly enrollment by age group until your projections show the center fully enrolled. Next, project your staffing month by month. Obviously, your staff will grow as your enrollment grows. However, for the sake of quality and to meet licensing regulations, you will have to hire your more expensive staff (fully qualified teachers) first.

Finally, break down your operating budget into a month-by-month format, prorated by the number of children projected each month. The result will be monthly operating losses until full enrollment. The total should be considered as part of the start-up budget so that the project is sufficiently capitalized.

WHAT IS AFFORDABLE TO PARENTS?

Most studies of child care costs have shown that lower-income families pay a much greater percentage of their incomes for child care than do middle income and more affluent families. The 1990 *National Child Care Survey*[3] reveals that families with annual incomes of under $15,000 spend 23 percent of their income on child care; families with incomes of $15,000 to $24,999 spend 12 percent; families earning $25,000 to $34,999 spend 8 percent; families with incomes of $35,000 to $49,999 spend 7 percent; and families with incomes of $50,000 or more spend only 6 percent of their income on child care.

In order to serve employees with the greatest need, develop policies for subsidized tuitions and explore sources of funding. Funding sources other than tuition must pay the difference between the tuitions set in the budget and the affordable tuitions paid by lower-income parents.

When developing a subsidy program, a tuition assistance program, or a scholarship program, it is recommended that subsidized employees pay approximately 12 percent of their family income for the child care tuition. When designing the program, consider such policy issues as income-level limits, income verification, confidentiality, and selection.

Once tuitions are set (based on the pro-forma operating budget), you can determine what level of family income is needed to afford those tuitions, using the 12 percent affordability factor. In looking at family income, look at all sources of income to the family. Child care centers often require a signed form in which the parent certifies that all income information is correct along with the latest paycheck stubs (see Figure 6.3). The confidentiality of this information must be maintained. Once an affordability scale is developed, a sliding tuition scale for parents can be devised.

Figure 6.3
Sample Scholarship Application

Date: _____

1. Child's Name: _____

   Address: _____

   Home Phone: _____ Date of Birth: _____

2. Mother's Name: _____

   Address: _____

   Employer & Address: _____

   Home Phone: _____ Work Phone:_____

3. Father's Name: _____

   Address: _____

   Employer & Address: _____

   Home Phone: _____ Work Phone:_____

4. List other children under 18 years (with ages) for whom you are financially responsible: _____

   _____

5. Custodial Parents' Gross Monthly Salary (before deductions and taxes are taken out):

   Mother: $ _____ Father: $ _____

6. Other Income:

   Child Support: $ _____ Alimony: $ _____

   Other: $ _____

This application is incomplete without an attached paycheck stub or equivalent verification of income from each custodial parent.

I certify that all statements and information given above are correct and authorize _____ to verify all statements.

Parent Signature: _____

Parent Signature: _____

Date: _____

This form (with verification) is required every six months.

Source: Based on a form used by Fairfax County, Virginia.

Here is an example of an affordability scale:

If tuitions are

$135 per week for infants
$120 per week for toddlers
$105 per week for two-year-olds
$95 per week for preschoolers

then at a 12 percent affordability rate, families must have the following gross incomes to afford the tuitions:

$58,500 per year to afford the infant tuition
$52,000 per year to afford the toddler tuition
$45,500 per year to afford the two-year-olds' tuition
$41,167 per year to afford the preschool tuition

Parents with gross family incomes below those levels would need a subsidized tuition. Please note, these tuitions are just examples and are low for large cities on the East and West Coasts, but high for the South and Midwest.

If you look at the family-income levels that are typical of the employees who may be using the center, or who you would like to encourage to use the center (to meet your goals of increased retention or lower absenteeism), you can determine the amount of subsidy that probably will be needed. Then you can create a sliding tuition scale (see Table 6.1). For example, the infant tuition is $135 per week. A family needs an annual income of $58,500 to afford that. You want to encourage some of your single parents who earn about $20,000 per year to use the infant center, but they can only afford $46 per week for child care. While the child of each of these parents is an infant, the parent would need a subsidy of $135 - $46, or $89 per week, to use the child care center. The required subsidy decreases as the child gets older, because the tuitions for older children are lower than those for infants. In looking at this example, please keep in mind that $135 per week is a low tuition for infants in a large East Coast city. A 1993 Catalyst study reported that average nationwide weekly tuitions are $113 for infants, $99 for toddlers, and $85 for preschoolers. The highest tuitions are $249 for infants, $186 for toddlers, and $162 for preschoolers.[4]

Table 6.1
Sample Sliding Fee Scale

Gross Income	Maximum Monthly Fee* for One Child Determined by Number of Dependents in the Family			
	1	2	3	4
8,500	62	38	15	0
13,500	112	88	65	41
18,500	162	138	115	91
23,500	212	188	165	141
28,500	262	238	215	191
33,500	312	288	265	241
38,500	362	338	315	291
43,500	412	388	365	341
48,500	462	438	415	391
53,500	512	488	465	441
58,500	562	538	515	491
63,500	612	588	565	541

*The monthly fees have been calculated by subtracting the federal tax exemption amount per dependent ($2,350), then multiplying by 12 percent, and finally dividing by 12 months. Nationally, it is generally accepted that budgeting 12–15 percent of a family's income for child care is considered affordable for most families.

WHERE CAN THE MONEY COME FROM TO SUBSIDIZE TUITIONS?

Some companies opt to subsidize a portion of the entire child care budget in order to lower tuitions for everyone, regardless of income. The company expenses are usually tax deductible as ordinary and necessary business expenses. Another source of funding may be state, county, or local jurisdictions. Your corporate child care center may be able to take advantage of available public funding for lower-income parents. Some jurisdictions have sliding fee scales in place for child care for low- and moderate-income families.

Your child care center can apply to be a part of the Combined Federal Campaign (CFC) if the center is a nonprofit corporation. CFC raises money through payroll deduction contributions from federal government employees. If there are a sizable number of federal government employees in your area who might contribute to the child care center, this is a good avenue of funding. United Way funding may also be a possibility. Check with your local United Way to learn the eligibility requirements. A local foundation may be interested in funding a special program in your child care center, which might free up some operating funds for scholarships.

Special fund-raising events can raise tens of thousands of dollars, or they can raise $250 and burn out all the volunteers. Concentrate on large events several times a year, and prepare a fund-raising calendar. Organizing these events takes many hours and requires a group of committed volunteers. Here are some ideas:

- Luncheon, dinner, or cocktail party hosted by a well-known person with a well-known speaker
- Silent auction
- Sales of plants, candy, calendars illustrated by children, or gift wrap, planned to coincide with holiday seasons
- Friends of the Center campaign—solicit contributions as "friend," "sponsor," "patron," etc.
- Walk-a-thon

Go for the big bucks. It is rarely worth the time and effort involved to raise a few hundred dollars.

WHEN DOES THE POEM REGAIN ITS BALANCE?

Let's look down the road a couple of years. Your center is fully enrolled. Your start-up costs were projected accurately. Your corporation has decided on a yearly subsidy to make child care affordable to all employees. The center is now humming along. There are no surprises. The corporation is not pouring money into a "black hole"; it is, rather, contributing a set and budgeted yearly amount for the purpose of affordability. Your center is a strong statement of the philosophy that young children need and deserve excellent quality care, and the whole project is a well-balanced piece of poetry.

NOTES

1. Personal correspondence with M. A. Lucas, September 9, 1993.

2. Committee for Economic Development, *Why Child Care Matters: Preparing Young Children for a More Productive America* (New York: Committee for Economic Development, 1993), 52.

3. Sandra L. Hofferth, et al., *The National Child Care Survey 1990* (study by the National Association for the Education of Young Children; Washington, DC: Urban Institute Press, 1991).

4. Catalyst, *Child Care in Corporate America: Quality Indicators and Model Programs* (New York: Catalyst, 1993), 51.

Chapter Seven

▨ ▨ ▨ ▨ ▨

Child Care Facility Design: More Than Building Codes

"Knock, knock."

"Hey, Sam! How're you doing?"

"Just a quick bit of info, Bob. I just had lunch with a friend of mine in Building and Maintenance. I mentioned child care to him and he said he knew nothing about it, but he did know that all construction must meet different codes. He lent me a copy of this BOCA* code book so I could see if it says anything about child care. And lo and behold, it does."

"That's a nice fat book, Sam. Looks like another area we need to investigate. This child care project is like archaeology! Do you think we'll find a Rosetta Stone at the end of our dig?"

Lynne Donges, manager of public affairs for the SAS Institute, says that the company's child care centers "create a triple win situation: our children win because they benefit from a quality environment that is conducive to healthy intellectual, emotional and social growth; parents win because their stress level is reduced knowing their children are getting quality care which

---

* Building Officials and Code Administrators

allows them to be happy, relaxed and productive. Finally the Institute is the big winner because those happy parents are dedicated, loyal and productive employees whose accomplishments contribute to the success of the SAS Institute."[1]

Therese Stratton, director of administration, Georgetown University Law Center, describes the Law Center's child care center this way:

> Many have told me their favorite place in the Gewirz Center is the child care center. It seems an oasis, a relief, a "fountain of youth" as it were in our high stress environment. There is such silliness in there, and imagination too. We have a wonderful blend of children and parents which include students, staff and faculty. The children are such a pleasant addition to our community. You see them chasing bubbles on the podium, tossing a ball on the lawn or setting up a lemonade stand on the quad, and you've simply got to smile.[2]

Fidelity Investments is part of a consortium that runs an emergency back-up child care center in Boston. Ann Andreosatos, director of employee benefit services, notes: ". . . 86 percent of the firm's employees who use the center would have had to stay home . . . there's an on-going return on our investment."[3]

We included these quotes so that you would remember that the end result can be well worth struggling with child care issues.

Now you know how to deal with the legal issues involved in starting a child care center, and you have a handle on what a child care center would cost. If you decide to go ahead with the development of a center—whether full-time, emergency back-up, or consortium—where are you going to put the little tykes? Read ahead; this chapter talks about site selection and space design.

WHAT DO WE NEED TO KNOW ABOUT SITE SELECTION?

Where are you going to locate your child care center? This is an important decision, which has many safety, programmatic, and financial ramifications. Here are some issues to consider as you decide "where to put the kids." Some of these issues are relevant only if you are going to build a new building for the child care center, others if you are going to renovate space in an existing building. These issues are also relevant if you are going to work with an existing center, because, in order to lessen your liability risk, you will want to be sure a center that you form a partnership with meets code and other safety requirements.

Size

The site should be large enough so that all children can be cared for on ground level. In many jurisdictions, this is a legal requirement for children under the age of two years. In any case, you must think about how all the children, many of whom may be infants and toddlers, can be evacuated in the event of a fire or other emergency. Eighty to 100 gross square feet per child is needed for construction purposes, excluding playground space. In addition, a minimum of 75 square feet per child (100 square feet is recommended), for children who will be outside at any one time, is required for a playground. Some city-based child care centers are able to use public parks for this purpose. We have compensated for the lack of playground space in some city-based centers by having centers use their own school buses to take children to different interesting parks and playgrounds every day.

Roads

For safety and security, the child care center should be set back as far from major roads as possible, while remaining easily accessible. High levels of exhaust fumes should not be present close to the playground. Of course, city-based centers are usually more limited in this regard than are other child care centers.

Circulation of Traffic

Analyze traffic patterns leading to and away from the child care center to avoid backups and dangerous intersections. There should be easy access to and from the main feeder road, with little impact on existing traffic patterns. Traffic circulation to the front door of the center should be in a one-way direction; a counterclockwise circulation to the front door will leave the passenger door next to the sidewalk. Keep in mind that the major traffic hours in and out of a child care center are usually between opening and 9 A.M., and between 4 P.M. and closing.

Parking

Adequate parking is needed nearby for staff, parents, and visitors. A stacking lane for drop-offs and pick-ups is especially important for arrivals and pick-ups during the peak hours. Local jurisdictions often mandate parking requirements. The location for pick-up and delivery of children should be as close as possible to the center's main entrance. Short-term parking spaces adjacent to the center are also necessary. City-based child care centers some-times do not offer short-term parking. In the city, parking is often up to the parents, and many use public transportation. Several drop-off and pick-up short-term parking spaces, however, are needed even in cities.

Pedestrian Access

Safe and barrier-free pedestrian access is needed from the parking area to the center. The walkways should be wide and well lit. Drop-off should be adjacent to the facility with no roads to cross.

Outdoor Lighting

The area around the center and parking should be well lit. The parking area is used early in the morning and later in the evening, when it may be dark.

Service Access

A loading area should be included in the outdoor space but away from the play area. Plan a place for food service, supplies, and equipment to be delivered. An enclosed dumpster pad should be located well away from the play area.

Architectural Compatibility

The child care center should blend harmoniously with the existing sur-rounding facilities and with any nearby residential areas. The center should also take advantage of natural landscape such as hills and large trees.

Future Expansion

Adequate planning and thought should be given to the potential for future expansion of the child care center.

Community Resources

Child care centers benefit from being located near community resources such as libraries, museums, nature areas, and interesting places of work. If the center is located in a city, there will probably be many community resources to enjoy.

Play Areas

Outdoor play areas must be located away from environmental hazards, such as aircraft noise, microwave radiation, and power lines. Review local codes for space requirements, keeping in mind that 75 square feet of play space per child should be a minimum. This does not mean that you must plan for 75 square feet times the number of children you expect to enroll. All children do not have to be outside at the same time.

Adjacent Uses

The existing and/or planned uses of adjacent sites should be compatible with child care center activities. Obviously, major hazards, such as large equipment areas and major power lines, should not be located adjacent to a center. Plan for your child care center to be located as far from your chemical research plant as possible!

Topography

Varied topography can create interest within the site. However, sites with too great a slope can be hazardous for young children and can create visual barriers for the staff. A civil engineer can discuss the construction issues of slope with you.

Soils

Soil bearing capacity affects the type of footings that can be used and thus the building development costs.

Utilities

Public utilities of sufficient capacity should be available. If storm water must be retained on-site in order to lessen the impact on downstream flow, a retention pond can be developed. This adds costs to the project, however, as well as another safety factor to deal with.

Vegetation

A variety of plant and tree species on the site may allow for a nature trail. Of course, no poisonous plants should be on the grounds of the child care center. This will be discussed later in this chapter in the section on playgrounds. Mature trees can be used as an architectural feature to shade the building and play areas. Vegetation also provides a noise buffer between the child care center site and adjacent properties.

Zoning

Be sure a child care center is permitted by right in your chosen location. If not, rezoning may be costly and time consuming. If you plan to renovate space within an existing building for a child care center, you still will have to meet certain regulations, such as having the number of exits required by the fire department. Even if you are not constructing a new building, look carefully at these site-selection criteria and use the ones that may be still relevant. For example, you must still be concerned about size, traffic patterns for drop-off and pick-up, parking, and playgrounds.

Emergency Back-Up Child Care Centers

Back-up centers, although small, need to comply with codes. Consider all the other issues discussed here in relation to back-up centers. Proper plumbing and electrical systems are needed to support all required bathroom and kitchen needs. A back-up center should also include a closed storage area.

WHY IS ARCHITECTURAL DESIGN SO IMPORTANT?

Architectural design is extremely important because it impacts the children's health and safety, social and emotional development, feelings of security and self-esteem, and learning opportunities. The environment is a critical part of the curriculum for young children. The child care center should be designed to give children opportunities to move freely, feel comfortable, and feel competent. A well-designed child care center offers people a variety of ways to use the space for many different activities. The environment should be more homelike than school-like and should combine adult-scale and child-scale components. Sinks, toilets, water fountains, and toy storage units should be scaled for a child's independence. Couches, chairs, rockers, diapering tables, and kitchens should be designed for the caregiver's comfort. Primary considerations in the design process include

- Homeyness
- Comfort
- Softness
- Security
- Safety

- Health
- Individual quiet space
- Social space
- Order

When possible, the design should include rounded walls and circular features, which produce a more cozy feeling than do sharp rectangular spaces. Individual space is as important as space for large-group activity. Children need small spaces to rest and observe activities, places where they can feel a sense of privacy.

The environmental decor should be low-key so that the children and their artwork, photographs, possessions, and activities are clearly the focal points of the center. Children are colorful—their clothing, toys, and art offer much bright color to the environment. Therefore, the background of the center (paint colors, wallpaper, carpeting) is best planned around a more muted color scheme. A calm background environment is more comfortable for both children and staff. Parents and staff truly appreciate entering a center that offers a homey, inviting atmosphere.

Soft chairs and couches, as well as carpeting (carpet squares are best for sanitary reasons), add to the homelike feeling. Shape patterns in the carpet add to the opportunities for children to play. We have seen children "fishing" over a large rectangular pattern in a preschool room carpeting, and we were warned to watch out or we would get our feet wet! Vinyl flooring in art, eating, bathroom, and diapering areas facilitates cleanliness. A variety of textures is important because the sense of touch is a critical sense for children, especially under the age of three.

All finished edges of construction must be rounded (including cabinets and sink counters), and there should be no projections (e.g., fire extinguishers and cabinets should be recessed).

The more natural light throughout the center, the better. If only one side of the building is exposed to natural light, try to design the play spaces on that side and use the interior space for support services such as offices, storage, and laundry and kitchen facilities. Variety in the architecture, such as areas for privacy and areas for groups, platforms, lofts, pits, climbing structures, skylights, trellises, and dividers, adds to the curriculum and the opportunities for imaginative play. Anita Olds, designer of environments for young children, advises that "varied minispaces prevent boredom, disinterest, and discomfort by enabling children to seek out activities and levels of stimulation to suit their moods and levels of arousal at different points in the day."[4]

Child Abuse Prevention

Child care centers can be designed to reduce the possibility of child abuse. First, adults should be able to see as much of the child care space as possible. An open space design, divided into child-sized group spaces by low half-walls or furniture, allows an adult to see and be seen by other adults throughout the day. Children feel that they are in small areas because of the placement of furniture and room dividers. Low walls seem like full walls to someone who is only three feet tall. Only the infant space should be a fully self-contained area. All other children's areas should be separated by low walls, gates, and furniture. This design supports interaction among staff and allows for continual informal supervision. Excess noise is kept to a minimum by the proper use and placement of sound muffling material.

Second, bathrooms should not have entrance or exit doors or doors on individual stalls. Young children have no need of such privacy. The bathroom area can be separated from the play area by walls with open entranceways so that adults can easily see into the bathroom if they wish. Ventilation can be achieved through the use of ceiling exhaust fans. Once children reach elementary school age, however, they do have a need for some privacy.

Third, any doors that do appear, such as doors to storage rooms, offices, staff lounges, or laundry rooms, should have large windows in them. Open space designs can serve to discourage people who are abusive from even applying for positions. In a center with no closed doors and with wide visibility, it would be difficult for child abuse to take place. Parents feel more secure leaving their children in centers where it is easy to see what is happening, and supervisors have a much easier job.

Very Large Centers

Centers for well over 100 children need special designs so that the very young children do not feel overwhelmed. If your center serves more than 120 children, you might consider subdividing your building so that children, parents, and staff feel that they are in a space and a program that is manageable in size. Two separate buildings joined by an administrative core, with one side for younger children and one for older children, may work well, or, as we would prefer, two minicenters, with all ages in each side so that children can be closer to siblings and so that they will see many of the same adults throughout their years at the center. Each minicenter should have its own entrance.

WHAT ABOUT LEGAL ISSUES?

In planning your child care center, you must work with an architect and a child care consultant who have experience designing child care centers. You also must meet all local and national code requirements. There are different requirements for buildings housing children under two years old than for children over two years old. In addition, all new construction and renovations must be designed in accordance with the Americans with Disabilities Act Accessibility Guidelines for Building and Facilities (ADAAG). The intent of the law is to provide "the most integrated setting appropriate for the needs of the individual." Program site requirements are included in ADAAG, as well as elements needed for access to the program, including sidewalks, doors, hallways, and restrooms. *Recommendations for Accessibility Standards for Children's Environments,* published in January 1992 by the Architectural and Transportation Barriers Compliance Board, lists details for construction. The Child Care Law Center also has information about the Americans with Disabilities Act and child care.[5]

WHAT ABOUT ALL THE DETAILS?

These are the types of spaces you will need:

- Lobby
- Reception/bookkeeper area
- Director's office
- Staff/resource room
- Infant care area (nursery)
- Toddler area
- Two-year-old area
- Preschool area
- Receiving kitchen
- Custodial room
- Storage
- Adult single toilets, including a facility for people with disabilities, plus one regular facility located in the infant area
- Laundry room
- HVAC/hot water mechanical room

There should be a minimum of 50 square feet of play space for infants in cribs and a minimum of 35–40 square feet of pure play space per child for toddlers on up. This translates into building at 80 to 100 square feet per child (the additional square feet go to hallways, storage, offices, bathrooms, and kitchens). Following are some things to consider for each specific space.

Lobby

The lobby sets the tone and atmosphere for the whole center, so it should look comfortable and inviting with a sofa, easy chairs, end tables, and plants. Children's artwork should be hung on the walls. Because the lobby will be the control point for all access to the center, it should open to a reception work area. The lobby is a good place for individual mail slots for each set of parents.

Reception/Bookkeeper Work Area

This area will serve two primary functions: staff can use this area both to accomplish the normal routine functions of the center and to monitor the coming and going of children, parents, and visitors. The reception area should include a workstation with a transaction countertop and one small office with windowed walls and a door for computer/bookkeeping work. Entrance to the work area should be closed off by a three-foot-high gate so that children can't get in but the receptionist can see them.

Director's Office

In this office, the director of the center can perform administrative duties and conduct small meetings with teachers and parents. This space should be constructed as a separate office with a door and have at least one glass wall from 30 inches above the floor to ceiling. Miniblinds or drapes will be required as window covering. The director's office can be built large enough for two desks if an assistant director is also required, or a separate assistant director's office can be constructed.

Staff/Resource Room

This is an informal lounge and work area where the staff can relax, take breaks, eat lunch, prepare materials, and have meetings. The staff room should have kitchen amenities and should be adjacent to a staff bathroom. This room should also include pigeonhole mail slots for teachers' mail, memos, etc.

Infant Care Area (Nursery)

Some people are horrified at the thought of infants in a child care center. These people have never seen a properly designed, high-quality infant center or nursery. The object of a well-designed nursery is to adapt the home-like environment so that small groups of children can be cared for, which is different from trying to make an institution less institutional. In designing a nursery, start with the aspects of the home that are desirable and adapt them to accommodate more children and health and safety necessities. In a home, there is a separate sleeping area, a separate play area, a kitchen, and a bathroom; these divisions are useful in the nursery as well. One large room, lit with bright fluorescent tubes, with cribs lining the four walls is not the way to go. Think instead of a diapering area, a kitchen area for food preparation and feeding, and a play space, not unlike a family room, with sofas, easy chairs, and a soft carpeted floor. Some wall lamps and decorations, and perhaps a large fish tank, finish a homey look.

Although the nursery is a closed, self-contained space, each infant area should be developed around an open environment plan, where there are no walls or partitions to block children and staff from sight. Infants need to be able to see their care providers whenever they wish, and adult visibility of all parts of the space is a must. Division of the nursery into playing, sleeping, eating, and diapering areas can be accomplished through low (36-inch) walls with peepholes and gates. A play space should be designed for six to 10 babies only, so, if your infant center has a large capacity, design several play spaces, separated from one another by the low walls with gates. The floor should be covered with carpet tiles, except in the kitchen and eating areas and in the diapering area. The nursery is the only children's area of the center separated from the rest of the center by floor-to-ceiling walls and doors, to reduce noise from the rest of the center. These doors and walls should have large windows. The nursery must be self-sufficient so that staff can provide full-time care. A staff bathroom should be located in this area. There must be adequate space for sleeping, feeding, crawling, active play, diapering, and nursing, and plenty of storage space. The nursery should be conveniently accessible from the lobby and adjacent to the toddler area. For fire evacuation, infants are rolled out of the center in cribs, so exits must be large enough to accommodate cribs.

Toddler Area

The toddler space also needs its own kitchen and diapering areas, but it does not need crib space, because toddlers can nap on little toddler cots, which can be stacked and stored in a closet when not in use. Lots of storage is needed in the toddler area. Play spaces should be designed for no more than eight children. Again, if capacity is larger, play spaces should be separated by 36-inch-high walls with gates or by furniture. This space should have a tiled "wet" area for artwork. The toddlers should be located close to a fire exit.

Two-Year-Old Area

These spaces should be self-sufficient, including sleeping, eating, and quiet and active play areas, so that staff can provide full-time care. Two-year-old areas should also include a diapering station, a children's bathroom, and a wet area for art. The twos' area can be designed as a large open area divided into two subareas with furniture or 36-inch-high walls with gates. Each play area can accommodate up to 12 children. These children love a little area, set away from the "madding crowd," where two or three children can relax, look at books, or just daydream. A loft designed for this age group is always a big hit. It is a good idea to include an open stall shower in the children's bathroom so that children can be "hosed off" if they happen to fall into a mud puddle or if bathroom accidents are really bad. Lots of storage is needed.

Preschool Area

This area will provide full-time care, including sleeping, eating, and quiet and active play, for three- to five-year-olds. Arrange the room into "learning centers" using equipment and furniture, and include lots of storage. A children's bathroom with gang toilets is needed, including one stall and a lavatory for preschoolers with disabilities. A "wet" area for artwork is needed.

Preschoolers love lofts. Lofts should be large enough for at least five children and simple in design so that children can use them in a variety of ways. The platform of a loft should not be more than four feet from the ground, and the floor of the loft should be carpeted. Stairs should be closed, with upright railings that are no more than one inch apart and four feet high on both sides. Railings should not give a toe hold for climbing. Children will also play in the space under the loft.

Receiving Kitchen

This area will be used to prepare snacks, to receive catered lunches, or to cook full meals. The kitchen should be located adjacent to a service entry. Plenty of storage and counter space is needed. Kitchen construction must meet local health codes, which are usually similar to codes for restaurants.

Laundry Room

A home-style washer and dryer is all that is needed. Most laundry is sent home to parents. It is also convenient to have a small stacking washer and dryer in the infant area for washing bibs and burp rags. The laundry room can be combined with the custodial room.

Emergency Back-Up Child Care Centers

If your back-up center is designed as one large room, be sure there is an area for infants that can be closed off from the rest of the center by a low wall or fence and gate. A crib area should be visible to the staff, but off to the side out of the main activity area. Diaper-changing facilities with a sink should be built in.

WHAT ARE THE GENERAL DESIGN REQUIREMENTS?

Following are general design requirements for child care centers.

Children's "Classroom" Areas

- Cozy areas for one or two children to play quietly away from the group.
- Varied levels—stages, pits, or lofts.
- Space with sinks for preparing and serving food.
- Easy access to bathroom, diapering areas, and sinks.
- Drinking fountain (for children over age two).
- General storage.
- Storage for each child's belongings.
- Telephone intercom system.
- Wall display areas.

Security

- A security analyst should assess center security and make specific recommendations.

- Consider intrusion detection at entrances and in the playground, remote-control door openings off the main entry and kitchen entry, and key card access.
- Consider a programmable keypad-entry lock system for the main entry door.

HVAC

- A separate HVAC system with 100-percent fresh air return is needed. Ventilate all spaces to accommodate the number of individuals per square foot.
- Add an extra quiet exhaust fan over diapering stations and children's and adult bathrooms. The fan should be on a separate switch from the lighting.
- Equip children's areas with individual controls to regulate temperature.

Electricity

- Incandescent lighting operated by dimmer switches is advisable in all children's areas. Dimmer switches should be mounted 48 inches above the floor.
- Full-spectrum fluorescent lighting should be used in all other spaces.
- All electrical outlets must be childproof and meet applicable electric code(s). Floor-mounted electrical outlets and any surface-mounted outlets and wiring (including telephone and other) are not acceptable. Mountings should be installed at a minimum of 40 inches above the floor.
- Dedicated outlets are needed for copiers and computers.
- There should be no outlets in the diapering areas.
- Outlets that are located near wet areas must be equipped with ground fault interrupters.

Telephone Equipment

- An intercom system should be installed throughout the facility, including the entry door, and centralized with several telephone lines at the receptionist's desk.
- All children's areas require a telephone system, which should have in-house service with an intercom system. Outside lines should only be on phones in the reception area, the director's office, and staff room areas. Several lines are needed.

- All of the rooms except for offices should have wall-mounted phones placed out of reach of the children. These phones should be mounted at a height of 54 inches from the floor.
- A facsimile machine is needed.

Plumbing

- The number of toilets and lavatories is controlled by state licensing regulations and local health codes. Toilets and lavatories must be child-sized.
- A minimum of one diaper-changing station with sink for every 10 children in diapers is recommended. Double stations can be designed with a shared sink in between. A group of young infants may need one diaper-changing station for every five infants. Sinks *must* be adjacent to diaper-changing tables.
- The number of adult toilets and sinks and bathrooms for people with disabilities must also follow codes.
- The drains in child-sized lavatories should be flush with the bottom of the sink and should not have the type of drain that pops up.
- There should be premixed tepid water (72–78°F) in all child-sized lavatories and sinks, as well as in sinks built in diapering stations.
- There should be cold water in the drinking fountains.
- Plumbing for a standard household-type washing machine is needed.
- Sprinkler protection is required as regulated by codes.
- An ice maker is needed for the refrigerator in each of the kitchens—in the infant-area kitchen and in the main kitchen.

ARE THERE SPECIAL REQUIREMENTS?

There are special requirements for child care centers. Following are specific considerations.

Ceilings

- Ceilings may include acoustical tile and height and lighting modifications, as needed for design.
- There should be acoustical ceiling tiles in children's spaces including children's bathrooms and diapering areas.
- Bathroom ceilings should be resistant to odor pick-up.

Wall Coverings

- Any vinyl wall coverings should be easy to clean and maintain. Wallpaper often adds a lovely homelike feeling to the lobby, offices, and staff rooms.
- Walls in the bathroom and food areas should be covered with epoxy paint.
- Other walls that are not papered should be covered with a minimum of two coats of hard, scrubbable paint that does not shadow or lose pigment when cleaned.
- Classroom areas should be painted so they can be cleaned more easily and so that artwork can be hung in more places.

Floor Coverings

- All classrooms should have vinyl tile and carpet squares (approximately one-third vinyl and two-thirds carpeted). The floor slab must be sealed, smooth, and clean before carpet installation.
- All bathrooms, kitchens, diapering areas, wet play areas, laundry, custodial, and storage areas should have sheet vinyl flooring.
- The lobby, reception/bookkeeper area, director's office, and staff/resource room should be carpeted.
- Floors should be carpeted with patterned interface carpet tile. Carpet tile is ideal for sanitation purposes, because a tile that is contaminated can be removed and cleaned or replaced. Carpeting also gives an opportunity for creative design. Sometimes basic shape patterns can be laid into the carpet with color so that children can use them for imaginative play.
- Exposed columns should be carpeted up to a height of 30 inches from the floor with broadloom material matching the floor carpet.

Window Coverings

- Windows should be covered with miniblinds or with fabric shades with pull-up reverse roll.
- All cords must be secured out of reach of the children.

Environmental Testing

- All of the standard environmental tests, such as tests for radon and for water impurities, should be run before construction.

Both new construction and renovations are governed by many federal, state, and local building codes. The ideas we have given here are supplementary to code requirements. We have included them because we know from experience that they work and that they are important.

WHAT DO WE NEED TO KNOW ABOUT PLAYGROUNDS?

Planning for outdoor play is an integral part of the design process for any child care development center. Outdoor play is important to a child's health and provides more expansive gross motor activity than is possible indoors. Through outdoor play, children can explore the environment, seek new challenges, and satisfy their developmental needs. A child care center playground can be a place where children can experiment with personal limitations and enjoy the freedom to run and play without traffic dangers.

Like indoor play, outdoor play should provide for the multiplicity of children's developmental needs. Most outdoor play areas support physical development quite well. A well-developed playground must, however, also support cognitive, creative, social, and emotional activities.

When selecting a playground site, there are several considerations. There should be a minimum of 75 to 100 square feet of outdoor space per child, based on the number of children who are playing outside at the same time. Survey the ground area to determine where all utilities are located underground and above ground; this will ensure that any proposed playground development does not interfere with the proper functioning of those utilities. The site should provide adequate protection from the sun and wind to make it usable during all seasons. Survey the drainage system and correct any problems before constructing play equipment. Investigate any hazards or obstacles to children traveling to or from the playground site. Ideally, the play area should be accessible only through the center and should be near restrooms and a drinking fountain.

The key to any playground is that it accommodates the developmental needs of all children. Each child should be able to enter a play situation at any level suitable for his or her own ability and needs. Plan for separate, but linked, play areas for children under two years old, two-year-olds, three- to five-year-olds, and school-age groups. Pathways with destinations and loops can be a major playground element, linking the various play areas. All play areas should be visible from the pathways so children can easily see and choose where they want to go. Enclosures of various types can be used to separate play areas. A combination of fencing, shrubs, seating, low walls, and level changes can be used. Young children require defined and protected play areas. Enclosed areas can help young children identify choices, but barriers should not block children's view.

Carefully consider preserving and incorporating all natural features, such as shrubs, trees, rocks, and hills, that will contribute to the play and learning of young children. Good landscaping can provide privacy and protection from the weather. Include a sand play area. Children at all developmental stages will find creative interests in building, digging, and measuring. This area should be exposed to sunlight for its sterilizing effects. Sand, however, does attract small animals, so there should be a way to cover the sand play area when it is not being used. Allow room for creative play, as well as areas for group games. Group areas should include places for outdoor art activities and places for quiet activities, where materials such as books and small toys can be used. The most valuable materials are those that children can move, build, tear down, rearrange, and use in creative play. Adequate storage facilities should be directly accessible to the outdoors for outdoor equipment. If children and teachers must carry everything outside for each play period, it is unlikely that a wide range of play choices will be available. Ideally, storage facilities should be located in each play area.

Successful playgrounds will include a variety of developmentally appropriate equipment and materials. Children's individual rates of physical development differ substantially, and a well-designed playground will accommodate those differences. For very young children, play equipment should be simple. With increasing age comes increased coordination, balance, strength, and ability to explore a much wider range of play equipment. Every playground should include places to slide, climb, skip, swing, balance, jump, run, throw, walk, explore, and pretend. Retreat areas such as platforms and forts should be planned for children to rest or watch. Plenty of "loose materials" are essential and provide a wider variety of play choices. Barrels, hula hoops, tricycles, parachutes, balls, blocks, short-handled shovels, buckets, sifters, and wagons are all examples of loose materials. Climbing superstructures should allow for a variety of exits, entrances, levels, linking parts, platforms, and activities. Clatter bridges, barrel slides, rope climbers, fireman poles, balance beams, flat platforms, pipe slides, wide slides, tire climbers, cargo nets, steps, and monkey bars work well with different age groups.

Well-designed playgrounds provide access to the area and the equipment for disabled children. An integrated playground will provide alternatives that permit children with disabilities and children without disabilities to play side by side. Specific design features such as the following should be considered:

- Handrails should be installed where appropriate, particularly on slopes.
- Provide easily accessible places for quiet activities.
- Avoid sharp corners or turns on pathways.
- Pathways should be made of a hard, smooth surface.
- Ramps should be used instead of stairs.
- Avoid using drain covers with slots that might trap wheelchairs.
- Design water and sand play troughs at wheelchair height.
- Equipment should not obstruct the movement of children.

Well-planned playgrounds will not only meet the developmental needs of all children, but will be designed to foster safety in all play activities. While it is important for children to take risks and challenge their physical abilities, they can also get hurt. Playground equipment is one of the major causes of injury for children. Two main sources of safety criteria for outdoor playgrounds are the U.S. Consumer Product Safety Commission's (CPSC) *Handbook for Public Playground Safety* and the Consumer Federation of America's (CFA) *Report and Model Law on Public Play Equipment and Areas.* Although compliance with both the CPSC and CFA guidelines is not mandated by law, safety experts consider the CPSC guidelines the very minimum required for safe play equipment and areas.

Following some basic safety precautions will reduce the chance that a child will be injured. A fence surrounding the playground will prevent children from inadvertently running into streets and will keep out any unwarranted visitors. The fence should be sufficiently high and constructed so that it does not invite climbing. Childproof exits are essential. Remove all toxic plants and replace them with safe materials. Plants are wonderful because they provide a natural setting and an important dimension for learning about the environment. Many common plants, however, are dangerous and even deadly. More than 700 typical plants in the United States and Canada have been identified as poisonous.[6] See Exhibit 7.1 for some commonly found plants to avoid.

Special consideration should be given to the safety of playground equipment. Safe "fall zones" consist of all ground areas under and surrounding all climbing and moving structures. Eight to 12 inches of wood chips, shredded rubber, or mulch in those areas will minimize or prevent danger in a fall. The higher the equipment in a play area, the deeper the recommended surface. All ground protection must be maintained and raked weekly to

Exhibit 7.1
Common Plants That Are Poisonous

Rosary Pea	Autumn Crocus	Columbine
Daffodil	Iris	Lily-of-the-Valley
Tulip	Tomato Leaves	English Ivy
Potato Vines	Laburnum	Laurels
Rhododendron	Azaleas	Yew
Wisteria	Morning Glory	Rhubarb Leaves

prevent packing and hidden hazards. Traditional metal equipment provides large-muscle activity, but can be dangerous. Metal is slippery when wet, hot in the summer, and cold in the winter. Wood or plastic-coated metal is recommended. All moving parts on play equipment should be made of soft material such as tires, ropes, nets, and canvas rather than metal, hard plastic, and chains. Ten to 17 feet of "run off" space is recommended at the end of equipment. Adequate space between equipment pieces will minimize children colliding into one another. Particular attention to swings is necessary. Excessive height is not necessary for play value or challenges and serves only to increase the potential for injuries. The highest platform of any structure should not exceed five feet or the reaching height of children. All openings or spaces that a child could possibly stick a body part through should be less than 5 inches or more than 10 inches in width. Commonly overlooked are openings between steps and rungs adjacent to the underside of a platform. Play equipment should be well maintained, with no protruding nails, splinters, sharp points, flaking paint, or broken parts. Particular attention must be given to the tops of slides, where loose clothing can get caught and cause strangulation. A safety inspection of equipment and grounds should be conducted on a daily basis.

Designing a playground that is safe for all children is critical. Appendix E lists sources of information on playground design and safety. Adult supervision, however, is an equally important factor. No matter how well planned a playground is, children will be injured if they are not properly supervised. The same staff-child ratios as recommended indoors should be maintained outdoors. Outdoor playtime should not be an opportunity for staff to socialize or sit under a shaded tree. All activity should be situated so that it is easily monitored. Staff should be stationed at each piece of stationary equipment in use and get involved, interact, and play with the children.

Once your indoor and outdoor space is complete—well-designed, safe, and inviting—it becomes a true haven in the corporate environment. As James Woolsey, director of Central Intelligence, remarked as he delivered a speech on the playground of the Langley Children's Center, "This is definitely the most enjoyable meeting I have addressed today."

> *How do you like to go up in a swing,*
> *Up in the air so blue?*
> *Oh, I do think it the pleasantest thing*
> *Ever a child can do!*
> *—Robert Louis Stevenson[7]*

NOTES

Thanks to Jim Dunlavey, principal, Einhorn, Yaffee, & Prescott, for suggesting the chapter title.

1. Lynne Donges, SAS Institute, as quoted in *The Corporate Reference Guide to Work-Family Programs* (New York: Families and Work Institute, 1991), 215.

2. Personal communication with Therese Stratton, November 2, 1993.

3. Carol Kleiman, "A Day Care Dilemma," *Chicago Tribune,* March 1, 1993.

4. Anita Rui Olds, "Psychological and Physiological Harmony in Child Care Center Design," *Children's Environments Quarterly* 6, no. 4 (Winter 1989), 11.

5. For more information, contact the Architectural and Transportation Barriers Compliance Board (Access Board), 1331 F Street, NW, S-1000, Washington, DC 20004-1111, (800) USA-ABLE; and the Child Care Law Center, 22 Second Street, 5th Floor, San Francisco, CA 94105, (415) 495-5498.

6. National Association for the Education of Young Children, *Healthy Young Children* (Washington, DC: National Association for the Education of Young Children, 1991), 48–50.

7. Robert Louis Stevenson, "The Swing," from *A Child's Garden of Verses* (New York: Macmillan Publishing, 1981).

Chapter Eight

■ ■ ■ ■ ■

Management: If We Do It, Who's Going to Run It?

"Hey, Bob. It's been a while!" David Stone grabbed his friend's hand and slapped him on the back.

"George has a way of keeping us all busy, doesn't he? Not much time for lunches with old pals!" Bob Roman frowned dramatically.

"May I take your order, gentlemen?"

"I'll have shrimp lemon grass soup and pud Thai with chicken, medium." David ordered.

"Grass noodle and seaweed soup and beef with Thai curry, hot." Bob turned back to David, "Either that will keep me alert for the afternoon or you'll have to call my gastroenterologist."

"Well, before I have to carry you out of here, Bob, tell me how your child care report is coming. Our next semiannual is in a couple of months. What do you think?"

"Almost done! I plan to send the report to everyone a month before the meeting so I can get your feedback. Surprisingly,

I've gotten some intermittent interest and support from George."

"Great!" David smiled. "I'm looking forward to seeing what you have to say. I know it's still an issue for a lot of people."

"Well, I do think we should at least do a needs assessment. We can see if the results corroborate the issues you found in your focus groups."

"All right! Great service, here." David breathed deeply. "This is a lunch befitting the standard bearers of human resources and quality."

So, who will run your hypothetical child care center? Yes, we know you do not want to be the one changing diapers. Once you learn a little more about early childhood development, you will understand what an important learning time diaper changing is, but we won't get into that now. You will need much more than diaper-changers, though, to run a child care center. A child care center is a small business and requires a person or a company with the knowledge and experience necessary to operate a small business.

You have several options for management of the center. (See Table 8.1.) You can hire an experienced director who will report to a designated person in your corporation or to a board of directors, depending on your legal structure. You can contract with a professional child care center management firm, which will provide an on-site director, staff, and all necessary support and enhancement of services. In this case, the management firm also will report to a designated person or a board. Another alternative is to contract with a local child care center to operate your center in addition to its other center(s). Finally, you can contract with a national child care center chain to operate your center.

The management option that you choose will depend on legal issues and the type of child care center your company wants to have. The amount of control and input you want will help you decide how the center should be managed. Your choice will also depend on what is available in your community. If your center is large enough, a large national chain would probably be interested in bidding on the project. If you have an excellent local child care center that wants to expand, that might be a good option. Maybe there is a child care center management firm that would like to run your center for you or a super person with an excellent reputation as a child care

Table 8.1
Who Are Running the Centers? A Sampler

Companies	Operating Source
America West Airlines Phoenix, Arizona	A local child care provider
Barnett Banks Jacksonville, Florida	A national child care chain
Blue Cross & Blue Shield North Quincy, Massachusetts	A local child care firm
Campbell Soup Company Camden, New Jersey	A local child care firm
First Atlanta Atlanta, Georgia	A local child care firm
Grieco Bros. Lawrence, Massachusetts	A director who reports to a board
Honeywell Minneapolis, Minnesota	A national child care chain
Lotus Development Corp. Cambridge, Massachusetts	A director who reports to a board
Milwaukee's Mitchell International Airport Milwaukee, Wisconsin	A local child care provider
San Francisco International Airport San Francisco, California	A director who reports to a board
Witchita Public Employees Wichita, Kansas	A national child care chain

center director available in your area. It is most cost effective for a small center (under 80 children) to look for a good, experienced director who can work on his or her own with some funding for staff and management training programs.

The selection of the person or firm to run the center on a daily basis is one of the most important decisions you will have to make. If you start off with excellent management, the center will be off to a fine start, full enrollment will occur on schedule, and the reputation of the center will spread, bringing with it accolades for your company. If, on the other hand, your initial decision does not work out, you will need to change managers, which will cause disruption.

How do you select a manager or provider? The selection process must be thorough and orderly for two major reasons. First, you want to be sure to carefully gather all possible information about your options so that you can make a well-reasoned, informed decision. Second, if there turns out to be a problem with the manager you have selected, it should be apparent that you exercised care and undertook a fair and thorough search for a qualified manager.

The best way to find an individual director is to advertise widely. You might solicit suggestions from your local Association for the Education of Young Children and from centers accredited by the National Association for the Education of Young Children (NAEYC) in your area. Place notices in local colleges that have early childhood programs as well as well-known colleges for early childhood education, such as Wheelock College in Massachusetts or Bank Street College of Education in New York City. Once you have a number of candidates, interview them thoroughly (your winning candidate should have had at least two in-person interviews), check references by telephone (written references are not enough), and run all the criminal records checks you can. The best way to select a management firm, a local child care provider, or a national chain is to issue a request for proposals (RFP) and then follow a detailed plan for review of the proposals received in response to the RFPs and selection.

WHAT GOES INTO A REQUEST FOR PROPOSALS?

An excellent question! In your RFP, you will ask for much detailed information, but you must start the RFP with a clear statement of what you want. The first step is to clearly identify your goals and objectives. Spell out who will oversee the manager, to whom the manager will report, and the relationship between the corporation and the manager or the child care center board of directors (if there is one) and the manager. What kind of oversight and control does your corporation wish to exert? Specify the financial commitment your company will make to the child care center and the quality factors that you will insist upon. The center should be required to begin the NAEYC's accreditation process by the third year of operation, if not before. Once you have a clear statement of your objectives and a clear description of how you envision the relationship between your manager and your corporation, you can list the information you want from your bidder. The information you request should include a capabilities statement, a description of the program philosophy and goals, and detailed descriptions of the program, including a budget. When you have developed a comprehensive RFP, your legal department should review it.

The capabilities statement should answer the following questions. What is the experience of the bidder? What other child care centers has the bidder managed? How long has the bidder been in business? How many people work in the company? Ask for an organizational chart of the bidder's staff and resumes of all employees who will be involved with the center. Who will be the key people involved? Who will be the center director, or how will that person be recruited? Bidders should be required to confirm that the key people noted in their proposal will actually be the people involved if their company is selected. The bidder also should submit financial statements, three letters of reference, and three telephone references who can be called.

The description of program philosophy and goals should clarify how the bidder's philosophy matches up with the accreditation standards of the NAEYC. The bidder should discuss a curriculum that empowers children to make decisions and follow their own interests; addresses all aspects of a child's development—social, emotional, intellectual, and physical; and discusses the child as an active learner, learning through play.

Each proposal should describe how the bidder envisions parent involvement and should emphasize an open door philosophy. The bidder should discuss communication as well as parenting education, including its formal mechanisms for communication such as a parent handbook, a center newsletter, a parent orientation process, and parent-teacher conferences. Informal methods of communication and opportunities for parents to be involved, such as parent volunteerism in the center and opportunities for short chats during the day, should also be described.

The RFP should request explanations of administrative procedures, including the procedures for enrollment, maintenance of waiting lists, marketing, tuition assistance, hiring, plans for staff retention, fire drills, evacuation plans, accident reports, security, quality control, and evaluation.

Ask that proposals include descriptions of staffing patterns and group sizes. You should mandate in your RFP the staffing patterns you want to ensure quality. How will staff-child ratios be maintained in the early morning and late afternoons when all the staff are not present? Ask how many part-time staff will be used. (If there are too many part-timers, there will probably be too much turnover!)

Descriptions of educational and experience requirements of staff should be included. Teachers should have four-year degrees in early childhood education. Assistants, at a minimum, should be high school graduates who have taken some early childhood classes in high school or community college. There should also be a definite effort on the part of the bidder to recruit a staff that is culturally diverse. Ask for descriptions of ongoing training programs for staff. There should be a structure for continuous feedback as well as formal training sessions throughout the year.

In the RFP, ask for descriptions of the child care center and program. If your manager will help you design the facility, you will want to know the design requirements for interior and playground. General descriptions of toys, equipment, and supplies that will be used are also useful. The materials should reflect the need for a wide variety of activities that the children can select on their own. The materials should also reflect the cultural diversity that exists in our society. Sample meal and snack menus should be provided. Make sure the snacks and meals are nutritious and meet USDA guidelines.

What policies will be established to ensure the health and safety of the children? What will be the policies and procedures for parents and staff? Ask for a sample parent handbook and a sample staff handbook. Make sure the policies reflect the philosophy stated. What insurance does the bidder hold and recommend for your child care center?

Finally, ask for a detailed, annotated sample budget for a center the size you are contemplating. Remember, they can't fudge it if you ask for a budget! Evaluate the budget carefully and weigh it heavily as you rate the proposals.

HOW DO WE FIND PEOPLE TO SEND THE RFP TO?

Ask your local branch of the NAEYC for a list of members, a list of local management companies, and suggestions of local centers accredited by NAEYC that might be interested in expanding.

Find out if there are other companies or government agencies with child care centers in your area and determine who is operating them. Ask the state and local licensing agencies and offices for children if they have any lists of child care centers or management companies that are interested in working with corporations. You can also ask for lists of managers and operators from Child Care Action Campaign, Child Care Information Exchange, and ACCCI: Society of Work Family Professionals. (See appendix G for the addresses of these organizations.)

HOW SHOULD WE EVALUATE RESPONSES AND MAKE A SELECTION?

We believe that the following is a thorough and logical plan to follow for selection of a manager:

1. Form a selection committee of three or five people.
2. Have each committee member individually read, carefully evaluate, and rank the proposals, with a ranking of one being the strongest.
3. Meet as a committee and reach consensus on the top three proposals.
4. Conduct interviews with the key people named in each of the top three proposals.
5. Narrow the selection to two candidates.
6. Visit child care centers run by the top two candidates. (See appendix H, Child Care Program Inventory (CCPI) Evaluation Criteria, for an evaluation form.)
7. Check references and do criminal records checks.
8. Make the selection.
9. Negotiate a contract with the winning candidate.
10. Use your gut instincts! Are these people you feel comfortable with? Are these people you can trust? Do you believe they are sincere? *Would you leave your children with these people?*

Let's repeat that last question. Would you leave your children with these people? These children will be adults, citizens, and employees very quickly. The early years set the stage for success in life, or for years of remediation or worse. Every child deserves a good start, so your decision about who will run your center is extremely important. Use your analytical skills to choose, but use your gut instincts, too!

Congratulations! You say you found a fantastic director for your center? She has a master's degree in Early Childhood Education and completed Wheelock College's graduate course in Day Care Administration? She has six years of experience running a child care center and wonderful references from board members, parents, staff members she supervised, and her professors. She is full of energy, very personable, and unswerving in her commitment to what is best for children. She is a whiz with numbers and loves budgeting. Grab her quick; she sounds like one of the rare gems!

And you? You found a wonderful company to run your center? Great! They have a curriculum coordinator and staff trainer to back up the director, as well as a financial manager to oversee the center bookkeeper. They have clearly spelled out systems for each aspect of operations and a wonderful record of recruiting fine directors for their centers. They will provide parenting seminars to all parents in the company, not just parents of children enrolled. They treat all the directors as a team so that they can support and learn from one another. Congratulations!

Chapter Nine

■ ■ ■ ■ ■

Special Tips: Nothing Succeeds Like Success

"Bob, Duncan Greenway on line one for you."

"Thanks, Alex . . . Duncan! What's up?"

"Hey, Bob. How's GO Systems' favorite child care specialist doing?"

"This is going to be one of our better reports, Duncan. Child care is a bigger thing than tricycles and teddy bears!"

"I have no doubt, Bob. But have you seen the giant teddy bear they put in Greenbaum's window at Christmas? Anyway, I am calling about my concerns about child care. You know I thought this could be a good marketing thing. But, did you see yesterday's Wall Street Journal?"

"I didn't notice anything about child care. Just skimmed it, though. What did it say?"

"There was this article—I'll send it over to you—about how most child care is not of good quality. If we do something, how will we guarantee that the quality is there? We'll lose any marketing opportunity if it's not good, and we could even get negative PR."

"Got a whole section on that, Duncan. Stay cool until you see the report. I definitely agree with your concerns."

"I didn't doubt you for a minute, pal. Your report will be my bedtime reading. Talk to you soon."

"Take care, Duncan."

HOW CAN WE ENSURE OUR CHILD CARE CENTER IS A SUCCESS?

If the center is set up correctly in the first place, in terms of policy development, physical space, and budget, you will be starting off on the right foot. The next step is to clearly understand who is responsible for what and what the exact roles of all parties will be. As we discussed in the last chapter, your decision concerning management of the center is extremely important. Once you have followed a thorough selection procedure and come to a hiring decision, you must negotiate a contract with your director, management firm, or provider. The contract should clearly delineate which responsibilities belong to management and which belong to the center's board of directors, or to your company if the center is not a separate corporation.

If the child care center is a separate corporation, the sponsoring company may wish to have a memorandum of understanding with the child care corporation, which clearly states the responsibilities of the sponsoring company and the responsibilities of the child care center. For example, such a document may state that the company will assume all space costs, including utilities, repairs, and upkeep to indoors and outdoors, such as lawn maintenance and snow removal. In a section listing center responsibilities, the document may state that the center must provide a program in accordance with the accreditation policies of the National Association for the Education of Young Children (NAEYC) and serve meals and snacks within the nutritional guidelines of the USDA. In this case, the sponsoring company, in essence, has a contract with the child care center. The child care center's board of directors then signs a contract with the management to run the center on a daily basis in a manner consistent with the memorandum of understanding. The clear delineation of responsibilities, both operational and fiscal, is the first step toward a smoothly running child care center.

Another crucial set of decisions for the success of the center is the hiring of the teaching staff, both teachers and assistants. These are the people who have direct contact with the children and who will have the most contact with the parents. The procedure for hiring, including interviews, reference checks, and background checks, should be developed before the child care center opens and should be included in the staff and parent handbooks. It is the center director's job to hire and fire staff in accordance with procedures approved by the center's board of directors or the sponsoring company. Sometimes the center's board will want hiring and firing decisions approved by the board's personnel chairman. This can work if the approval process is timely and does not slow the process. There is a child care staff shortage in the country, so delays in the hiring process can cause a center to lose good potential staff people. Please remember that proper hiring is critical to the long-term success of the center. Just hiring "warm bodies" to watch the children so that enrollment can rise more quickly is a serious mistake and will be detrimental to the center in the long run. Sponsoring companies and center boards must remember this when pressure is on to increase enrollment and cut operating shortfalls.

Ongoing management training for the center director is another underpinning that should be in place to help ensure success. The center director's job is extremely difficult because it calls for so many different skills. The director must be an excellent communicator, a public relations person, a supervisor, an early childhood education expert, a financial manager, and a crackerjack administrator. It is, needless to say, difficult to find one person with all of these skills, so ongoing training in skills directors lack or need to improve is essential. A management firm or a nationwide chain probably has its own internal director training programs. If you hire a director to work alone, however, you must plan for director support and budget for it.

We have already mentioned, in chapter 5, the importance of comprehensive written policies. These policies must be gathered into parent and staff handbooks and discussed thoroughly with each incoming family and each newly hired staff person.

A quality assurance plan is obviously a key to avoiding problems. Who will be the troubleshooter? Who will perform periodic evaluations of the program? If you contract with a firm or provider for management, be sure regular internal evaluations will be undertaken. If you have a director, it should be part of his or her job description to evaluate regularly. In any case, management should also undertake a formal annual evaluation of the center, with questionnaires for parents and staff. Sample evaluation forms can be found in appendix H.

Public relations also must be emphasized. Key people in the sponsoring company must be kept apprised of the center so they recognize its importance to the company. Monthly newsletters and annual reports should be sent to these people, and briefings should be requested at least semiannually. Public relations is also important for building enrollment and keeping the center at capacity. Nothing is more important for marketing than positive word of mouth. Sometimes people think that if their center is at capacity enrollment and there is a waiting list, nothing needs to be done in the marketing arena, but continual attempts to build goodwill for the center will be like money in the bank when the center needs something special or when company demographics cause a temporary enrollment dip in a certain age group. A continual nourishing of positive public relations by the child care center will also pay off in employee support for the center, even among employees who do not use it. The center will be a source of pride for all employees. The importance of goodwill holds true for any type of child care option you may choose.

The need for proper financial management systems cannot be overemphasized. A system must be in place for the production of monthly financial statements, statements of budget deviations, and cash flow projections. There are commercial software packages on the market for child care center financial management. Some sponsoring companies take care of financial management for their child care centers. The center finances should be audited by a CPA yearly. In addition to being a proper management technique, the yearly audit is required by some public and nonprofit funding organizations.

HOW CAN RELATIONSHIPS BETWEEN A CENTER BOARD AND THE DIRECTOR BE KEPT SMOOTH?

For child care centers that are organized as separate corporations with a center board of directors, board-director or board-management/director relations can be the greatest pitfall. Sometimes when there are board-director disagreements, the director is fired or quits and the center is left in disarray. How can this be avoided?

First, director-board relationships can be difficult for several reasons. A child care center is a very emotional place. The director is usually someone who has very strong opinions about what is best for children. The child care profession is greatly undervalued by society, however, and this sometimes leads to defensive behavior on the part of child care professionals. You may have a director who is passionate about what children need and, at the same time, somewhat touchy about criticism or disagreement with his or her positions.

The board members, for their part, have an enormous amount of responsibility on their shoulders. Their decisions affect many children and many parents who are employees of your corporation, and often the board members do not know a lot about child care. For these reasons, they may be extremely cautious and fearful of making mistakes, embarrassing the corporation, and perhaps endangering their professional status. An overly fearful board interacting with a defensive director is a recipe for conflict.

There are several things that can be done to avoid problems. First, the board should not be too large. Five to 11 people works best, with larger centers having nine to 11 board members and smaller centers having five to seven board members. Too large a group makes it difficult to gain consensus on issues, and consensus is a better method of decision making than voting. Also, too large a group leads to "dead weight," people who do not contribute and who often skip meetings. These people can demoralize the workers on the board, and also make it difficult to maintain a quorum.

Second, the makeup of the board is very important. The qualifications of board members and the method of selection are two key elements to think through. Board members must be open-minded people with no specific "ax to grind." If they are parents, they must always consider the broad picture of the child care center, rather than the issues that concern their particular child. The board should be broad based, composed of people with a range of talents. You may want to include a lawyer, someone with a financial background, a marketing person, a person with fund-raising experience, and a person with strategic-planning experience. Board members should be at least as diverse as your corporation in terms of gender, age, and race.

The method of selecting board members should be described in the center bylaws. In some centers, the board elects new board members to fill expired terms. In other centers, the child care corporation solicits parents and other interested employees to run for election, and the members of the corporation elect the board members. The founding board is usually appointed by the sponsoring corporation and serves until elections are held, as described in the bylaws. It is a good idea to retain the founding board for a year after the center opens. Appendix I is an example of an application for board membership. Table 9.1 shows the National Center for Nonprofit Boards' recommendations for board composition for a hypothetical organization.

Table 9.1
Hypothetical Board Composition

Key Dimensions for Board Members: Community Organization of Greater Nonprofitsville																		
Dimensions	Current Board Members											Potential Members						
Age	1	2	3	4	5	6	7	8	●	●	●	A	B	C	D	●	●	●
Over 60	●			●		●	●											
45-60		●	●					●										
Under 45					●													
Sex																		
Female	●	●	●			●	●	●										
Male				●	●													
Race																		
Asian																		
Black	●			●														
Hispanic						●												
White		●	●		●	●		●										
Geographical Location																		
City	●	●	●		●	●	●											
Suburbs				●				●										
Area of Expertise																		
Administration							●											
Finance		●																
Fund Raising		●	●															
Business	●																	
Legal								●										
Marketing						●												
Planning																		
Public Relations				●	●													
Organizational Experience																		
Business	●	●					●											
Government			●		●			●										
Nonprofit				●		●												

Source: Reprinted from National Center for Nonprofit Boards, *The Chief Executive's Role in Developing the Nonprofit Board*, Nonprofit Governance Series No. 2 (Washington, DC: National Center for Nonprofit Boards, 1990). (202) 452-6262.

Next, the responsibilities of the board must be clearly understood. The board deals with the development of policy through a committee structure and with fund-raising. The Board *does not* deal with the daily operations of the center. Richard T. Ingram has described the 10 basic responsibilities of nonprofit boards:

1. Determine the organization's mission and purposes.
2. Select the executive.
3. Support the executive and review his or her performance.
4. Ensure effective organizational planning.
5. Ensure adequate resources.
6. Manage resources effectively.
7. Determine and monitor the organization's programs and services.
8. Enhance the organization's public image.
9. Serve as a court of appeal.
10. Assess its own performance.[1]

The responsibilities of the center director must also be clearly understood. The center director must be the voice for appropriate curriculum and practices. The director must be a strong person, because he or she must be the center of information in the child care center and serve as a gatekeeper of information flow. Board members who need information about an aspect of operations must ask the director. Parent concerns must be relayed to the director, either by the parents themselves or by the staff. Staff concerns must be brought directly to the director. The director is responsible for everything that happens each day and must be careful to document all occurrences and conversations of substance. The board has a right to know about everything that transpires, so the director has a responsibility to inform through regular (we suggest monthly) written reports to the board.

The director and board must have the same goals. In general, the goal should be to provide an outstanding early childhood program to the children enrolled while making every effort to meet the needs of the working parents of your company. What if the board thinks that accommodating all employees' needs is paramount, even if it means keeping the center open 18 hours a day and being flexible about staff/child ratios so that more children can be added as the need arises? What if the director thinks that it is not good for children to be at the center for more than eight hours a day, and that exceptions can never be made to ratios? You will have conflict.

The board and the director must respect the structure of the center and the offices of the director and the board. The director must understand and respect the board's right to know and provide the board with comprehensive monthly reports of activities, problems, and concerns. The board must not micromanage and must allow the director to do his or her job.

The director and the board must trust each other. Trust takes time to build and comes with experience, as both the director and board see that the other will do its job competently. While trust builds, the relationship must depend on mutual respect.

A team approach is essential. The director and the board must work as a team. It is important to understand that on a team players do not step on one another; rather, they know and play their own clearly defined positions, and each player adds to the success of the team.

There are eight common pitfalls to avoid:

1. A director who withholds information from the board.
2. A director who does not do his or her job, for example, a director who does not support staff through feedback and training or does not communicate well with parents.
3. A board that micromanages.
4. A board that is apathetic, continually puts off decisions, or does not follow through.
5. Communication that does not follow proper channels. The board should not discuss issues with the staff or the parents without going through the director. Neither should the staff or parents have direct access to the board. Communications must go through the director.
6. A board member who dominates to carry out a personal agenda.
7. Power struggles between board members that deadlock a board.
8. A director and board with different goals.

You will not fall prey to these pitfalls if everyone is aware of them in the beginning, the board members are professional in their work, and the director is competent and respects the board's responsibilities. Formal board training programs and retreats can be extremely helpful.

WHAT IS THE ROLE OF THE DIRECTOR AND/OR MANAGEMENT?

The director's administrative duties include maintaining licenses, certifications, and insurance policies by ensuring that requirements are met on a daily basis and renewal procedures are instituted at the proper time. Directors must also maintain systems for staff hiring, child enrollment, children's movement through the center as they age, and parent communications. As mentioned above, directors must maintain systems of communication with the board or corporate liaison. Daily evaluations of the environment, staff, and children must take place for risk management and troubleshooting reasons.

Some of the director's financial responsibilities are ensuring that financial procedures, including systems for checks and balances, are followed; expenditures and income remain consistent with the budget; financial projections are produced as necessary; and monthly statements are accurate and timely. The director must supervise the bookkeeper and communicate regularly with the center's treasurer if the center is set up as a separate corporation.

The director is responsible for staff training and curriculum development. Ongoing training, both formal and informal, is essential. Health and safety evaluations of the physical plant and staff procedures must be performed daily.

Parent communication is extremely important. Systems for daily, weekly, and monthly communication, both written and oral, must be in place and followed. Parenting education is also important for the center to sponsor. The director is also responsible for informally assessing children and suggesting to parents resources for meeting any special needs of their children. The director must also think in terms of strategic planning and be prepared to present new strategies to the board, or corporate liaison, for consideration.

It's quite a job, isn't it? That is why you must have training and a support system in place for the director.

NOTE

1. Richard T. Ingram, *Ten Basic Responsibilities of Nonprofit Boards* (Washington, DC: National Center for Nonprofit Boards, 1990).

Chapter Ten

■ ■ ■ ■ ■

A Note to Small Businesses

The vast majority of businesses in this country are small businesses. That means there are a lot of employees needing family-friendly policies and programs! Small businesses can benefit from increased public relations, reduced turnover, and enhanced productivity as well (see Table 10.1), and a lot of them already know this. In a 1991 report, the Child Care Action Campaign cataloged various models of child care options undertaken by small businesses.[1]

Small businesses often face special problems when attempting to implement family-friendly benefits. The most obvious one might be a tighter budget, less money to expend on new projects. Small businesses might also have staff limitations; everyone is so busy doing the work of the business, no one has the time to develop a new program. Since they probably do not have a large in-house legal staff to deal with problems, small businesses might also think that they must move more cautiously.

Nevertheless, small businesses are providing family-friendly benefits with many of the same successes as larger businesses. In fact, many small businesses find it easier and more natural to be flexible and implement these benefits because the owner knows each employee, the large bureaucracy does not exist, and communication is uncomplicated. As Virginia Fisher, human resource director for the 40-person International Trans-Script company, has said, "In many ways these [small] employers are more sensitive than large ones. They're small enough that they can say 'This is what we need to do to retain this very talented person.' "[2]

Table 10.1
The Five Smallest Companies in *Working Mother*'s 1993 Top 100 Companies

Companies	Employee Size	Flexible Work Options	Child Care	Elder Care	Benefits
		Family-Friendly Options			
G.T. Water Products, Inc. 5239 N. Commerce Avenue Moorpark, CA 93021	26	Flextime. Part-time.	On-site free year round school. Before/after school, holiday, and summer programs, and sick care. Sick child days.		Savings plan. Phase-back new mothers. Adoption aid. Baby gift.
Tom's of Maine P.O. Box 710 Railroad Avenue Kennebunk, ME 04043	80	Work at home. Job sharing. Flextime. Compressed work weeks. Part-time.	Funds community child care programs. R&R. Sick child days. Subsidies.	Resource and referral.	Savings plan. Phase-back for new moms. Adoption aid.
Frontier Cooperative Herbs P.O. Box 299 Norway, IA 52318	172	Work at home. Job sharing. Flextime. Part-time.	On-site center. Holiday, summer, and back-up care. Sick child days.		Savings plan. Phase-back for new moms. Tuition reimbursement. Wellness plan.
The John D. and Catherine MacArthur Foundation 140 S. Dearborn Street Suite 1100 Chicago, IL 60603	184	Job sharing. Flextime. Compressed work weeks. Part-time.	R&R. Sick child days.	Resource and referral.	Savings plan. Tuition reimbursement. Phase-back for new moms. Adoption aid.
Calvert Group 4550 Montgomery Avenue Suite 100 North Bethesda, MD 20814	191	Work at home. Job sharing. Flextime. Compressed work weeks. Part-time.	Child care subsidies. R&R. Sick child days.	Resource and referral.	Savings plan. Long-term care insurance. Tuition reimbursement. Phase-back for new moms. Adoption aid.

Source: Based on information from Milton Moskowitz and Carol Townsend, "100 Best Companies for Working Mothers," *Working Mother* (October 1993), 27–66.

WHAT OPTIONS DO SMALL BUSINESSES HAVE?

Small businesses must undertake the same kind of research as larger businesses in order to select the best child care option for them. So conduct your needs assessment and then consider the following options, which work especially well for small businesses.

Direct Services

- Join with other businesses in your immediate area to form a consortium to develop a full-service child care center or an emergency back-up child care program. Consortia are very workable for small businesses, because costs and spaces are shared. A company that does not have enough demand to warrant its own program may well have enough demand to be part of a consortium. Appendix B lists consortia composed of both large and small businesses. Government agencies and law firms have been especially active in forming consortia. Some of the resulting programs are full-service child care centers; others are emergency back-up centers.

- Along with other businesses, develop a "warm line" for children who are home alone after school to call for reassurance, information, and homework help. A group of businesses might approach a community center, YMCA, county agency, or religious organization to determine whether it would be interested in operating a business-funded "warm line." This is one example of how valuable partnerships can be for small businesses.

Alternative Work Schedules

- Develop policies that allow flextime, telecommuting, part-time work, and job sharing.
- Revise personnel policies in some of the ways described in chapter 2. Allow leave for school conferences and events.

A small business might have trouble implementing some typical alternative work schedules. For example, if too many people chose a 5-4-9 schedule (see chapter 2 for explanation), there might not be enough people at work on Fridays to keep the business going. On the other hand, in a small business employees can sit together, discuss problems, and brainstorm solutions. Barbara Belfie, an employee of Washington Dental Service, is extremely grateful for her company's flextime policies: "Now if my kids are sick, I don't get nervous about calling in. Management understands and is willing to work with me."[3]

Financial Assistance

- Begin a Dependent Care Assistance Program (IRS Section 129).
- Develop a voucher program.
- Implement a baby bonus.
- Develop a discount program.

Maine Antique Digest has had a voucher program for more than 10 years. Co-owner Sally Pennington notes that 14 of her employees have been with the company for more than 10 years, and she attributes much of this retention to the voucher program.[4]

Education and Information

- Sponsor a seminar series on work-family issues.
- Sponsor parenting and elder-care support groups.
- Put on a work-family resource fair.
- Develop a work-family resource center.
- Distribute a work-family newsletter.

Employees have a tremendous need for information, and they do not have the time to do thorough research on their own. Simply supplying employees with lists of sources of free and low-cost information with addresses and phone numbers is a valuable service. There are many free resources from national associations. For example, the National Association for the Education of Young Children has a wealth of information on selecting quality child care and on parenting issues. Organizations and their phone numbers are listed in appendix G. State licensing offices also may publish helpful information (see appendix D). On the elder-care side, the national Elder Care Locator, a free resource that can help employees find assistance for aging relatives across the country, is available by calling (800) 677-1116.

Seminars, usually held during lunch hour, are also greatly appreciated. Some well-received topics include dealing with a sick child, finding school-age child care, supporting children who stay home alone, coping with sibling rivalry and teenagers, defining quality child care, disciplining children, communicating with caregivers, balancing work and family, accessing elder care resources, and planning ahead for elder care.

Monthly support groups are also welcome on issues such as parenting preschoolers, dealing with teenagers, and caring for elders. Support groups should be led by experienced facilitators.

An on-site resource center that stocks relevant articles, books, pamphlets and brochures, magazines, and videos is a godsend to many employees. The resource center coordinator may also be qualified to offer some individual counseling to employees in need of specific services.

Community Investments

Investing in even one community-based child care center to provide needed technical assistance to improve programs or administration or assist with accreditation is extremely worthwhile. If employees happen to use the center, the benefits to the company will be even greater.

Other Options

- Distribute pagers to expectant fathers.
- Set up a lactation room for nursing mothers.
- Put together new-parent information packets.
- Establish reserved parking for pregnant employees.
- Donate car seats for new babies.
- Create a toy lending library.

Small businesses can move faster, be more individualized in their approach to problems, and, in return for individualized attention to employee needs, receive greater loyalty from their employees. Don't hesitate. Start to plan!

NOTES

1.   Caroline Eichman and Barbara Reisman, *Not Too Small to Care: Small Businesses and Child Care* (New York: Child Care Action Campaign, 1991).

2.   Marilyn Gardner, "Big Ideas from Small Companies," *Working Mother* (January 1994), 35.

3.   Ibid, 40.

4.   Martha Michaels, "Small Companies Help Parents Balance Job and Family," *Office Advisor* 2, no. 3 (Fall 1993).

Chapter Eleven

■ ■ ■ ■ ■

"An Invasion of Armies Can Be Resisted, but Not an Idea Whose Time Has Come"

"Good morning, all!" George Oliver smiled as he strode into the board room. "Thank you for your concise reports in preparation for our meeting today. You have all made important progress on the goals we set six months ago. Before we get into production issues, I'd like to deal with a subject that I have found to be surprisingly intriguing—the report on child care that Bob and his people put together. I know several of you had input into this one, and I want to thank you for your thoughtfulness. Larry, you and your legal staff must have had some fun with this. A far cry from your usual work load, wasn't it?"

"Right, George. I hadn't thought about the liability of tripping on teddy bears before!"

"Well, seriously though, I have always believed in family values—believed that we need to provide as well as we can for our children—but I'm beginning to think that my idea of

family may be a bit outdated. I have received quite an education about this lately, both from your report and from my daughter. Some of you may not know that my daughter, Alison, is six months pregnant with my very first grandchild!"

"Here! Here!" The group raised their coffee cups in a toast.

"Thank you. Thank you. Well, Alison and Bob's report have convinced me that we should at least do a needs assessment and see what the employees' child care needs are. And I do appreciate all the detailed information you've included, Bob, so that we know up front the issues that we may have to deal with. You've all had a chance to read the report. What are your reactions? We can take 10 minutes for this."

George is right. Things have changed. In 1970 there were 18 million two-income households. Today there are 31 million.[1] Twenty percent of families are headed by a single parent, and 4 percent of those single parents are dads.[2] Moms and dads are both working and need flexibility in the workplace. "I can get work done here in three or four hours that would take me all day down there because of all the interruptions," an employee of the Washington, DC, office of the General Services Administration said. This worker used to spend three hours a day commuting to and from work. He now commutes 15 minutes to a telework center.[3] The Traveler's Insurance Company has found that offering telecommuting gives the company a tremendous advantage in recruitment and retention.[4] People want to take advantage of new technologies such as telecommuting so that they can be more available to their families and avoid long commutes in clogged traffic.

Changes have come to the work force as well. White males no longer dominate the work force and are projected to be among the minorities of the work force by the year 2050. The work force today is a diverse composite of men and women of many races and cultures. After the recession and massive layoffs of the late 1980s and early 1990s, people no longer believe that their companies will take care of them throughout their working lives. The company man is defunct. On the other hand, companies know that turnover costs an average of 1.5 times salary, and they realize that they must work to retain valuable employees.

Child care. Elder care. Work-family. Family-friendly. Flextime. Telecommuting. Job sharing. Glass ceiling. Equity. Total quality. Diversity management. Indeed, the times have changed. But these buzzwords are parts of a diversity snowfall that is blanketing the landscape and creating new land-marks for corporate executives. Those businesses that embrace this new landscape and take advantage of its assets will see increased profitability.

Two truths emerge as the corporate community and the country as a whole look at goals for the beginning of the twenty-first century. First, our educational system must change. (See Exhibit 11.1.) The system must pro-duce better-educated citizens and workers, and the system must naturally begin with child care. Second, we must embrace the diversity that com-prises this country and its work force and recognize diversity as value added.

Exhibit 11.1
What Has Happened to Our Educational System?

- As many as 25 million adults are functionally illiterate.
- American students rank near the bottom in math and science achievement when compared with other nations.
- Approximately 1 million students drop out of high school each year.
- Another 700,000 high school seniors will graduate, but will be as deficient in skills and work habits as most dropouts.
- Less than 50 percent of high school seniors read at levels adequate for understanding moderately complex tasks.
- Thirty-three percent of 11th graders are unable to write a co-herent paragraph about themselves.
- Nearly 35 percent of 8th graders are unable to figure the cost of a meal from a menu.
- Eighty-five percent of 8th graders cannot solve simple math-ematical problems involving fractions, decimals, percentages, or simple algebra.
- Approximately 35 percent of kindergarten children come to school unprepared to learn each year.
- While the number of students in schools in the United States has remained the same, total spending for elementary and secondary schools has more than doubled since 1980.

Source: Facts were obtained from *The State of America's Children 1992,* devel-oped by the Children's Defense Fund, Washington, DC 20001, and *Children in Need: Investment Strategies for the Educationally Disadvantaged,* developed in 1989 by the Committee for Economic Development, New York, NY 10022.

This diverse work force includes a large number of people with child care problems.

Many are alarmed at the current state of education in the United States. At an address to the annual conference of Business for Social Responsibility in October 1993, Lester Thurow, who at the time was dean of the MIT Sloan School of Management, asserted that we are creating a third world inside our first world, and this situation is making it impossible for the United States to compete successfully in world markets. Secretary of Labor Robert Reich, at the same conference, also expressed concern about the education of our children. Approximately one million students drop out of high school each year. Another 700,000 graduate but are as deficient in skills and work habits as most dropouts. Not even 50 percent of high school seniors read at levels considered adequate for understanding moderately complex tasks, and 80 percent have inadequate writing skills. American students are mediocre at best in international comparisons of mathematics skills and rank near the bottom in international science achievement. Students in the United States are also extremely weak in history and geography.

At the same time, unskilled laborers are no longer in demand. The technological revolution has brought jobs that require more literate workers with problem-solving skills and teamwork know-how.[5] Companies in the United States are finding themselves responsible for educating their own employees. Large and small companies across the nation have had to begin literacy programs. Motorola, for example, even started its own "university" to educate its employees. Aetna Life & Casualty provides training to entry-level workers in reading, writing, and oral communication skills.[6]

At the 1992 Children's Defense Fund conference, Secretary of Labor Robert Reich noted that education begins at birth, not age six, and quality child care has great implications for later learning. The Child Care Action Campaign has undertaken a multiyear project, Child Care and Education: The Critical Connection, to eliminate the barrier between the care and education of children. The objectives of this campaign are to foster the understanding that quality child care and education are part of the same process; to ensure that the child care needs of children and parents are addressed in the education reform agenda; and to make the vision of a continuous system of child care and education a broadly supported public policy. John Goodlad, director of the Center for Educational Renewal at the University of Washington in Seattle, asserts, "We need something different, and what we need is a massive early childhood support system, massive early childhood education. We're never again going to get that nice neat family we like to talk about with so much nostalgia."[7]

A solid early childhood education, which must be delivered by the child care system for the nine million children in child care, is essential for school readiness, the first of our National Education Goals, which were set by President Bush and the nation's governors in 1991. The reality of 70 percent poor-quality child care in this country must be a clarion call to all sectors of society to join together to solve this problem. Business, government, and parents must all demand for and plan for the emergence of a steady supply of high-quality care for children in the United States. Child care is extremely important because it impacts the future of all of us. Future members of our work force are receiving their educational foundations today, and poor child care cannot provide the proper educational start for children. Businesses need to lend their resources to the struggle of the child care community and local, state, and federal governments to improve child care quality. Honeywell has initiated a project called Success by 6, which was designed to prepare children to be successful in kindergarten. The United Way of Minneapolis led this endeavor and coordinated the efforts of business, government, labor, education, and health and human services.[8] Businesses that begin their own high-quality programs, as well as those that work to enhance existing programs, help themselves in terms of both preparing a future work force and reaping the benefits of improved recruitment, retention, and public relations today.

In addition to their educational role, child care programs play an important role in meeting the needs of a diverse work force. Thirty-eight percent of the work force is comprised of working parents. These parents represent one aspect of the diverse work force for employers to consider. As these parents strive to be responsible employees as well as responsive parents, they greatly appreciate employer-supported child care programs and reward their employer with loyalty and increased productivity.

WHO MAKE UP THE DIVERSE WORK FORCE?

The diverse work force is sometimes viewed as a challenge for employers, but businesses that view a challenge as an opportunity for growth are the types of businesses that have always been successful. It is the goal of employers to help each employee become as productive as he or she can be. Accepting and, more importantly, capitalizing on diversity leads to a more committed and productive work force. At the 1993 Businesses for Social Responsibility conference, Paul Fireman, CEO of Reebok International, spoke about diversity as a business opportunity. He urged businesses to "seek out people with new and different stories to tell. . . . Greet diversity and welcome it." He noted that a Hispanic employee had the idea for Reebok's first successful shoe. Another success of Reebok was the new idea that women needed special shoes. He summed up the decision to make special types of women's shoes like this: "Some made a choice to hang on to yesterday rather than grab on to tomorrow."

The American work force of today is composed of men and women of all races, religions, ethnic backgrounds, and nationalities, and we expect this to be true for the work force of the future as well. Diversity management traditionally refers to embracing the potential of people of all racial and ethnic groups, but we submit that diversity management can be thought of in a broader context.

A diverse work force includes employees with young children who may at times be distracted from work by child care and parenting concerns; employees with teenagers who may be concerned about their children's whereabouts in the afternoons when school is out; and employees who are struggling to pay college tuitions. Some of these employees may be single moms or single dads who have no one with whom to share their concerns. In addition to child care concerns, employees may have responsibilities for elderly parents or other relatives. The work force also includes people who are coping with illnesses or disabilities, either their own or a loved one's, while they fulfill their work obligations. Adding to the diversity are employees who are of Hispanic, African American, Asian, Eastern European, Middle Eastern, or any other background who find themselves bridging two cultures. Many employees do not speak English as their first language, and many are not part of the dominant American culture. Women employees who are trying to enter top management are part of the diverse work force, as are white males who, of course, want to be treated fairly. Companies must also consider employees who enter the work force poorly educated with limited experience in problem solving and teamwork.

ISN'T THIS DIVERSE WORK FORCE A MAJOR PROBLEM FOR EMPLOYERS?

The poor education of some entry-level workers is certainly a problem, as we have discussed. But the other components that make up the diversity of the work force are not problems; they are just the opposite. If your business works to maximize the potential contributions of diverse people, it will reap the rewards of the creative ideas of a committed and loyal work force.

Managing diversity is not the same as complying with equal opportunity or affirmative action guidelines. Managing diversity means embracing the potential of each employee for an improved bottom line. It is about not wasting people. It is about being flexible enough to take into account employees' diverse needs for the end result of increased productivity.

Stephen J. Inman of the Society for Human Resource Management EEO Committee member, notes, "Managing diversity involves recognizing that different people can and will make similar contributions to an organization in very different ways and that it's OK for people to be different and perhaps they should not always be treated exactly the same."[9] The Kaleel Jamison Consulting Group explains, "A group of people excited by their differences and willing to share them communicate on a necessarily sophisticated level. . . . Listening across areas of difference means being able to project beyond one's own sphere of experience. Such listening skills allow an organization an advantage with customers . . . and enhance internal problem solving and decision making."[10] Ann Morrison of the Center for Creative Leadership adds, "If the work force is changing, the customer base is changing. . . . The evolution of what were niche markets—Hispanic, Asian, and African-American—into very large mainstream markets is the compelling force that's causing a lot of executives to say, 'We need to pay attention to this. We need to do something about it.'"[11] Ethnic-minority shoppers spent $600 billion in 1992, up 18 percent since 1990. By the year 2000, minorities may account for 30 percent of the economy.[12]

A totally white male corporate power structure will have a hard time dealing with the reality of a diverse work force and a diverse customer base. Managing the diversity in the work force requires different kinds of support structures and benefits and, most of all, flexibility in dealing with employee needs in order to foster their development as productive and contributing employees. Secretary of Labor Robert Reich says that "there are two kinds of companies: those that think people are assets to be developed and those that think people are costs to be cut. Research has shown that in the long run, the high performance companies are those that help people to be more productive." At a conference in July 1993 in Chicago on the Future of the American Workplace, Philip Condit, president of the Boeing Company said this: "Technology can be copied and moved readily. If we are going to win, it will be because of the assets of our people, and those people working together are absolutely crucial to our future." At the same conference, Robert Haas, chairman and CEO of Levi Strauss, asserted, "The real technology of the 1990s and the 21st century is our people."[13]

Managing diversity, then, is managing business's most important asset—people. As a business community, we have been attempting to do this
in various ways for over a decade. These efforts have often been successful
and have led to more productive employees. The earliest efforts toward
helping employees realize their potential were perhaps the Employee Assistance Programs. Total quality management (TQM) efforts began in the
1980s as another effort to maximize employees' productivity. The awareness of gender equity issues such as glass ceilings are again an effort to
maximize each employee's potential. Work-family programs are set up to
assist employees with child care and elder care problems so that their productivity can be improved and their potential can also be fully realized.
Concerted efforts to recruit people of color and an emphasis on cultural
diversity are another effort not to waste human potential. We live amidst
diversity of all types. Businesses that take advantage of diversity by recruiting all types of people and then providing programs and policies that
will support this diverse work force in various ways will be rewarded with
a work force that understands the customer, because the customer is not
only the stereotypic middle-class, middle-aged white male. Figure 11.1
shows how we see it fitting together.

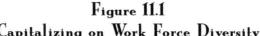

Figure 11.1
Capitalizing on Work Force Diversity

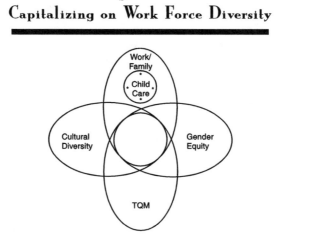

Child care, as you can see, fits in as part of a work-family program.
Many companies that started with child care programs have expanded their
programs to assist employees with other dependent care needs. Elder care

programs, which offer information and resources to employees struggling to care for older parents or other relatives, are valuable programs for a segment of the employee population. Work-family programs often stress flexibility in personnel policies and benefits so that employee needs can be met to some extent throughout the life cycle. Adoption benefits, parental leave, child care programs, college advisory services, elder care referral services, workshops and support groups, newsletters, and resource fairs have all been adopted by companies in an effort to ease the employees' burdens of integrating their work and family lives, so that they can be more productive employees. One small copying company, composed of mostly single people, purchased a washer and dryer for use during the day!

Why is child care marked with asterisks inside the work/family circle? Because child care is a most important component of work-family. Children have only one childhood in which to develop the self-confidence and character to become positive, productive citizens of the future. A large proportion of children spend many hours each day in child care programs. It is up to all segments of society—parents, business, and government—to see that in their earliest, most crucial years they receive the care and stimulation needed to get them off to a good start. Arnold Hiatt, chairman of the Stride Rite charitable organization, explained the involvement of his company in child care in this way: Children who get a "good early start . . . become tax payers instead of tax users. Prevention costs less than rehabilitation. . . . It costs $8500 per year for day care. It costs $32,000 per year for rehabilitation for a teenager."[14]

The goal of corporate-sponsored child care programs is to help enable parents of young children to use their potential fully, without the distractions of child care problems. The goal of each work-family program is to enable employees to maximize their potential. TQM, gender equity, and cultural diversity programs have basically the same goals as work-family programs: to provide supports and eliminate barriers so that the full potential of the work force can be realized. If products and technology can be copied and improved upon, then truly the only stable asset to business is the brain power of its people. Employees will develop new ideas, new products, and new technologies. Businesses must empower their employees to do the best job they can. This does not mean that businesses will have to provide the same supportive programs and benefits for each employee, but businesses will have to provide diverse programs to meet diverse needs. Helen Mills, president of the Mills Group and cochair of Businesses for Social Responsibility, states it clearly: "Companies that don't view their relationship to their employees as one of symbiosis will become extraneous to the mainstream marketplace. Developing, facilitating and promoting workplaces that accommodate family-friendly realities will create and nurture the highly productive symbiotic employer/employee bond."[15]

The white male is not to be forgotten in all the emphasis on diversity, since he is indeed a part of the diverse work force. It is likely that he will appreciate work-family programs as much as anyone, given the realities of family life as we enter the twenty-first century. Michael S. Kimmel, in a *Harvard Business Review* article, put it this way: ". . . today's company man carries a briefcase while pushing a baby carriage."[16] In December 1993 the *Washington Post* ran an article about two high-level presidential advisors who were quitting. In discussing the toll his long work hours took on his family, Roy Neel, deputy White House chief of staff, said, "I realized that I'd become more and more irrelevant to the operation of my family."[17] The societal change is profound.

WHAT ABOUT EQUITY?

How can we provide policies and programs that might benefit one group in our diverse mix of employees but not everyone? Let's look at the benefits that impact most people today. You subsidize parking spaces for employees, but I use public transportation to get to work. You subsidize food in the company cafeteria, but it is still too expensive for me, so I bring my lunch. You have a beautiful fitness facility, but I cannot come in early to use it or stay late because I have to drop off and pick up my children at child care. You have an employee assistance program, but I fortunately have never had to use it. You offer free financial planning seminars, but my brother is a financial planner. These corporate benefits are all valuable and excellent, but not every employee can or does partake of them equally. To this list we might add wellness programs, stress management seminars, stock purchase programs, and retirement planning. The point is that policies and programs that are available now are not meeting everyone's needs equally. It is impossible to meet everyone's needs equally in a diverse work force. However, if a variety of programs, including work-family programs, are offered and are packaged as a comprehensive work-life strategy, the equity issue disappears.

A second equity issue often arises around benefits for multisite companies. One answer to this concern is to decentralize programs so that they make sense for each site. Analyze the work-family needs of employees of each site separately so that the resulting programs work for each locality. Sallie Mae, with eight sites nationwide, and Champion, with 15 major sites, have both taken this tack for their many work sites. Doris McGhee, vice president of human resources for Sallie Mae, explains: "From a business standpoint, we realize that to be effective, the work-family programs at each of our locations must meet the needs of the employees at that site. It doesn't make sense to offer the same programs throughout the company in the interest of equality if these programs don't address employees' needs. To determine local employee issues and concerns, we conducted an in-depth needs analysis at each of our work sites."[18] Another example is Fannie Mae, which has developed an emergency back-up child care center for its national offices in Washington, DC. For employees in each of its five regional offices, it has set aside emergency child care vouchers for $25 per day for up to 20 days per year, which roughly equals its subsidy for the child care at the national office.[19]

WHAT IS THE CURRENT STATUS OF WORK-FAMILY PROGRAMS?

Families and Work Institute[20] has done much research on the evolution of work-family programs in companies. In general, many companies start with an isolated child care program to help meet the needs of working parents. The program might be an on-site, near-site, or consortium child care center; a resource and referral program; or the institution of a DCAP. Some companies have then moved to a broader work-family program that encompasses some elder care services. Personnel policies are often revised to reflect the needs of the employees for greater flexibility. At a later stage, work-family issues become linked with other corporate initiatives such as diversity management, gender equity, and total quality.

Companies have often become stymied, however, in the implementation of new policies and programs because managers have not bought into the new programs. Employees may say that what is on paper is not what is instituted. Often these managers are people who have struggled to move up in the corporation under the old systems, which did not acknowledge work-family issues. Now these people are asked to be flexible and understanding to their subordinates. Sometimes the managers have not felt the personal impact of work-family struggles.

Educational programs and training are essential. Work-family training for managers should include

- the demographics of today's work force and the current work force of your corporation

- the bottom-line benefits of work-family programs
- the importance of maximizing each employee's potential
- a review of all work-family programs in place in your corporation
- problem solving and listening skills
- techniques for managing flexible schedules, including evaluating output rather than time spent in the workplace
- awareness of one's own attitudes
- a review of what other companies are doing
- the integration of work-family with other company initiatives such as TQM or diversity management
- the clear commitment of the CEO to work-family programs

If the CEO and top management are clear about the value to the company of work-family programs, that message has to be reinforced for managers down the line. Work-family training and implementation of programs and policies are taken more seriously when they are tied to a manager's performance evaluation and incentives. Managers must be trained to evaluate output instead of hours spent in the workplace. Work-family programs will meet their goal of maximizing employees' potential only when employees actually use them, and employees will use them only if they know that the policies are supported by their supervisors and that their promotions will not be stymied if they do take advantage of available programs.

IS IT A MISTAKE TO START WITH ONE SMALL PROGRAM?

No, indeed. Do your needs assessment and start with the greatest need. You now know what your choices are. Whether you make your policies more flexible, develop a work-family resource center, develop a full-service child care center, sponsor a seminar series, start a local fund for child care support, or make some other change, you are contributing to the well-being of your employees, their children, and your business. It is a win-win situation. The only caveat is this: whatever you do, do it right. We do not need any more poor-quality child care in this country. Your company can be part of the child care solution while you enhance your bottom line with more productive and stable employees.

"Mr. Oliver, your wife is on line one."

"Yes, dear?"

"George, I'm at the airport. Annie called and said your mother fell and broke her hip. I spoke to the doctor and he said she'd be fine, but she'll be in the hospital for a while. I should get there by 4:00 P.M. our time. I'll call you when I get to the hospital. George, we may really have to think about relocating her this time."

All of us have families of some kind. All of us who work must figure out how to integrate our work and family lives so that we are as productive as possible on the job and as responsive as possible to our loved ones. It can be done. It takes the commitment to break old paradigms. It takes an attitude of teamwork between management and employees at all levels. It takes the understanding that today's work force and customer base are diverse, with diverse needs, and that this also will be true in the twenty-first century. It takes flexibility and creativity and vision. Go for it! The rewards are there for our businesses, and, in order to ensure continued prosperity, our responsibility to America's children cannot be shirked. Here is Richard Stolley's analysis:

> American companies have resisted helping employees with child care for several reasons, some dumb, some short-sighted, most of them wrong.
>
> First, a frontier feeling that work and family should be kept separate, a 19th century philosophy that our global competitors overcame long ago.
>
> Second, a fear that child care will be too expensive, but that does not factor in the cost to American business of absenteeism, distraction and turnover caused by poor child care—$3 billion a year for absenteeism alone, CCAC has estimated.
>
> And third, a worry over liability. And yet, trained providers and affordable insurance can take care of that false alarm.
>
> In the end, American business has resisted child care because its reluctance mirrors a peculiar American attitude toward children in general, especially young children. It is an attitude of savage ambivalence. We are sentimental about our country's children, but in our actions we do not value them. We say we love them, but we give them little honor.

This is not to say that American business does not respond to calls of conscience. It does, acknowledging a moral imperative to improve the lot of the disadvantaged, including children, both with charitable dollars, volunteer efforts and, sometimes, business-government partnerships.

But if the child care crisis is to be solved—and I define solution as nothing less than quality, affordable child care for every American family that needs it—then corporate response will have to go well beyond what we can expect from appeals to business leaders' conscience.

They must understand that they, and their nation, are paying a fearful price for our national failure to care for and educate our youngest generation. They must acknowledge that child care, and other family friendly policies, will play a crucial role in the development of a work force in this country that can successfully compete in the fierce battle for economic dominance. And finally they must consider the irrefutable evidence that helping with child care will help their bottom line, that doing good in this case is the way to do well.[21]

NOTES

1. "Number of Two-Income Households Grows," *National Report on Work and Family* 6, no. 22 (Nov. 24, 1993), 8.

2. Committee for Economic Development, *Why Child Care Matters: Preparing Children for a More Productive America* (New York: Committee for Economic Development, 1993), 5.

3. Stephen C. Fehr, "Moving the Job Closer to the Commuter," *Washington Post,* September 26, 1993, B1.

4. Patricia L. Mokhtarian, "Telecommuting in the United States: Letting Our Fingers Do the Commuting," *TR News* 158 (January–February 1992), 2.

5. Committee for Economic Development, *Children in Need: Investment Strategies for the Educationally Disadvantaged* (New York: Committee for Economic Development, 1989), 5.

6. Robert H. Rosen, *The Healthy Company* (New York: Putnam Publishing Group, 1991), 155.

7. Gelareh Asayesh, "Ten Years After A Nation at Risk," *The School Administrator* 50, no. 4 (April 1993), 8–14.

8. Diane Gingold, "American Corporate Community Service: Time to Act," *Fortune Magazine* (November 30, 1992), 12.

9. "Work Force Diversity: What It Is, How It Should Be Managed and How to Harness Its Full Potential," *Human Resources Management—Ideas & Trends in Personnel,* 7 (newsletter published by Commerce Clearing House, Chicago, IL).

10. Catherine S. Buntainee and Frederick A. Miller, "Building Diversity in the Workplace: Good Values—Smart Business" (presentation at the Businesses for Social Responsibility Conference, Washington, DC, October 22, 1993).

11. Sharon Nelton, "Winning with Diversity," *Nation's Business* (September 1992), 19–24.

12. Thomas McCarroll, "It's a Mass Market No More," *Time* (Fall 1993, special issue).

13. U.S. Department of Labor, "Wake-Up Call for Investors," *American Workplace Newsletter* 1, no. 1 (September 1993).

14. Presentation at the Businesses for Social Responsibility Conference, Washington, DC, October 21, 1993.

15. Personal correspondence with Helen Mills, December 14, 1993.

16. Michael S. Kimmel, "What Do Men Want?" *Harvard Business Review* (November–December 1993), 50–63.

17. Lloyd Grove, "Fire in the Belly, Then Heartburn," *Washington Post,* December 9, 1993, D1.

18. Personal correspondence with Doris McGhee, vice president of human resources, Sallie Mae, June 1993.

19. Personal conversation with Gene Ritzenthaler, director of employee benefits, Fannie Mae, June 1993.

20. Families and Work Institute, Ellen Galinsky and Dana Friedman, copresidents, 330 Seventh Avenue, New York, NY 10001.

21. Personal correspondence with Richard B. Stolley, senior editorial advisor, Time, Inc., May 31, 1994.

Appendix A

Executive Summaries

CHAPTER 1

- Family-friendly companies receive much free publicity.
- The work force has changed:
  More diverse
  More female
  More dual-career families
- The work environment is changing:
  Organizational charts are being revamped
  Employees are increasingly valued for their input
  Emphasis on teamwork
  Sensitivity to family issues

- Benefits of family-friendly policies include
  Increased productivity
  Reduced turnover
  Improved quality
  Reduced stress
  Improved recruitment
  Increased employee morale and job satisfaction
- Decision makers must consider the next generation and the future work force:
  Support for early childhood education is needed
  Corporate involvement is essential

CHAPTER 2

Direct services include

- On-site/near-site child care center
- Consortium child care center

- School-age programs
- Emergency back-up care
- Family child care provider networks

- Sick-child care programs
- Weekend/evening care

- Transportation

Alternative work schedules include

- Flextime
- Telecommuting
- Personnel policy changes

- Job sharing
- Part-time work

Financial assistance options include

- Voucher system
- Vendor or discount system
- Flexible spending account (DCAP)

- Baby bonuses
- Subsidies for child care expenses related to travel or overtime

Education and information services include

- Resource and referral systems
- Seminars, workshops, and support groups
- Resource fairs

- Resource libraries
- Working-parent newsletters
- Supervisor training

Community investments may include

- Seed money for expansion of existing programs
- Recruitment campaigns for family child care providers
- Technical assistance for staff training, director training, or board development
- Scholarship money for children from low-income families

- Money to begin a transportation program for school-age children
- Accounting and legal assistance
- Fund-raising assistance
- Salary subsidies

CHAPTER 3

A child care decision should be targeted to the following two goals:

- Easing the specific company problems that are attributed to child care issues

- Easing the most glaring child care problems of the employees

A comprehensive needs assessment consists of four parts:

- Examine company's goals and corporate culture and look at any problems from the company's point of view.
- Assess the employees' needs through focus groups and a needs assessment survey. Reducing response bias, assuring a high response rate, and making sure the right questions are asked will ensure a successful needs assessment survey.
- Perform a market study of available child care.
- Compare the data you have gathered to the child care options that are possible for your company.

CHAPTER 4

- A child care center that enrolls infants to five-year-olds will need about 80 children for financial viability.
- Generally 2–3 percent of an employee population in a large, diverse work force can be expected to use a company-sponsored child care center at any one time.
- Many companies subsidize the yearly operating costs of their centers from one-third to one-half of the budget so that tuition fees are affordable and the program is high quality.
- A feasibility study should include
    An analysis of all parts of the needs survey
    Site analysis
    Projected budgets
    Risk factors
    Options for organizational structure
    A time line and scope of work for development of the project if a decision is made to go ahead
- The development of a child care center includes tasks associated with
    Program design
    Architecture
    Playground
    Security
    Finance
    Permits and licensing
    Founding board/steering committee
    Board calendar and agenda items
    Equipment and supplies
    Insurance
    Administration
    Center calendar
    Marketing
    Food service
    Staffing
    Staff training
    Transportation
    Parents
    Children and enrollment
    Curriculum
    Moving in

Opening week
Community liaisons
Grand opening
- Quality will depend on
  Child/staff ratios
  Group size
  Educational level of staff
  Staff salaries
  Ongoing training programs

A well-educated and
  experienced director
Ample equipment and
  supplies
A safe, clean environment
An open-door philosophy for
  parents

CHAPTER 5

Options for the legal structure of a child care center include

- A department of the
  corporation
- A wholly owned subsidiary
- A separate nonprofit
  corporation

- A contract with an outside
  group
- A consortium child care center

Liability and how to limit risk:

- Get insurance:
  Bonding
  Comprehensive general
    liability
  Directors and officers
  Excess liability coverage
  Student accident coverage
  Vehicle
  Worker's compensation
- Remember that state licensing
  regulations are a floor, not
  necessarily an indication of
  quality
- Attend to physical design
- Develop thorough policies and
  procedures

- Stress teamwork among staff,
  parents, and management
- Develop careful staff hiring
  procedures and policies
- Institute ongoing staff training
- Attend to security of all
  children through carefully
  developed policies and
  procedures
- Insist upon an open-door policy
  for parents
- Ensure that the program is of
  high quality

CHAPTER 6

Start-up costs include

- Construction
- Equipment and supplies
- Personnel
- Insurance
- Operating losses

An operating budget should cover

- Salaries and benefits
- Possible space costs
- Food
- Management or consultant fees
- Staff development
- Employee relations
- Repairs and maintenance
- Office supplies
- Curriculum supplies
- Center supplies
- Insurance
- Field trips
- Professional fees: legal and accounting
- Transportation
- Advertising
- Miscellaneous
- Contingency
- Replacement reserve
- Shortfall

Sources of income are

- Tuition
- Enrollment and application fees
- Fund-raising
- Interest income
- USDA
- Possible corporate subsidy

Ways to provide affordable child care:

- Provide subsidy
- Fund a sliding fee scale

Sources of funding for subsidized tuitions are

- Corporations
- State, county, or local jurisdictions
- Combined federal campaign
- United Way
- Foundations

CHAPTER 7

In selecting a site, consider

- Size
- Roads
- Traffic circulation
- Parking
- Pedestrian access
- Outdoor lighting
- Service access
- Architectural compatibility
- Future expansion
- Community resources
- Play areas
- Hazards
- Adjacent uses
- Topography
- Soils
- Utilities
- Vegetation
- Zoning

In designing a child care center, address

- Children's emotional and social development
- Learning opportunities in the environment
- Health and safety issues:
  Rounded walls
  Finished edges of construction
  Open space/open bathrooms
  Half doors

Plan for space for

- Lobby
- Reception/bookkeeper work area
- Director's office
- Staff/resource room
- Infant care area
- Toddlers area
- Two-year-olds' area
- Preschool area
- Receiving area
- Laundry area

General requirements include

- Multiuse "classroom" areas
- Security requirements
- HVAC specifications
- Electrical specifications
- Telephone/intercom
- Plumbing for toilets, lavatories
- Diaper-changing tables
- Ceiling specifications
- Wall covering
- Floor covering
- Window coverings
- Environmental testing

In planning playgrounds, attend to

- Site selection
- Design features

- Safety requirements
- ADA requirements

CHAPTER 8

Options for management of the center:

- Hire an experienced director
- Contract with a professional child care center management firm

- Contract with a local child care center or organization
- Contract with a national child care chain

Selecting an individual or management firm:

- Advertise widely
- Interview thoroughly and check references by telephone

- Issue a request for proposals (RFP) to select a management firm or a child care provider

What to require in an RFP:

- Capabilities statement
- Philosophy and goals
- Description of parent involvement
- Administrative procedures
- Staffing patterns and group sizes
- Educational and experience requirements of staff
- Ongoing training program for staff

- Design requirements
- Description of toys, supplies, and equipment
- Sample meal and snack menus
- Description of policies and procedures for parents and staff
- Health and safety policies
- Insurance
- Sample budget

Locating people to send the RFP to:

- Contact local branch of the National Association for the Education of Young Children (NAEYC)
- Determine who is operating local employer-sponsored child care centers

- Contact state and local licensing agencies and Offices for Children
- Contact child care associations

Evaluating responses and making the right selection:

- Form a selection committee
- Interview and check references

- Visit centers run by the top candidates

CHAPTER 9

How to ensure success within the child care center:

- Develop a specific contract with director or management
- Develop a memorandum of understanding between the corporation and child care center
- Follow careful procedures in hiring the teaching staff
- Ensure ongoing management training

- Ensure that comprehensive written policies are followed
- Implement a quality assurance plan
- Emphasize public relations
- Follow financial management systems

The board/director relationship:

- Consider the size of the board, which should be 5 to 11 people
- Carefully consider the makeup of the board
- Delineate board responsibilities
- Delineate director's responsibilities
- The board and director must have
    The same goals
    Respect for the offices of the board and the director
    Trust for each other
    A team approach
- Avoid common pitfalls:
    The director withholds information from the board

The director does not do his or her job
The board micromanages
The board is apathetic
Communication does not follow proper channels
One board member dominates to carry out a personal agenda
Power struggles between board members deadlock a board
The director and board have different goals

The role of the director and/or management firm:

- Administrative
- Financial
- Staff training and curriculum development
- Parent communication

- Assessment of children
- Health and safety
- Strategic planning for board presentation

CHAPTER 10

Direct services may include

- Forming a consortium to develop an emergency back-up child care center

- Developing a "warm line" for school-age children

Alternative work schedules may include

- Developing policies that allow flextime, telecommuting, part-time work, and job sharing

- Allowing leave for school conferences and events

Financial assistance options may include

- A dependent care assistance program

- A voucher program
- Baby bonuses

Education and informational services may include

- Seminars
- Support groups
- Resource fairs

- A resource center
- A work-family newsletter
- Workshops

Investments in the community may include

- Providing technical assistance for staff training, accreditation, or director training

Additional options may include

- Pagers for expectant fathers
- Lactation room for nursing mothers
- New-parent information packets

- Reserved parking for pregnant employees
- Car seats for new babies
- Toy lending library

CHAPTER 11

- The education system in America is failing:

  A child care system is the first step in the education process

  A strong early childhood support system is needed

  Corporate involvement should be expanded

- The diverse work force is a reality and an asset:

  A large portion of the diverse work force has child care concerns

- The goals of all work-family initiatives are to provide supports and eliminate barriers so that the full potential of the work force can be realized.

- Equity issues will disappear when a broad work-life framework is described.

- Work-family training for managers is an essential part of program implementation.

Appendix
B

■ ■ ■ ■ ■

Partial Listings of Employer-Supported Child Care

PARTIAL LISTING OF COMPANIES WITH EMPLOYER-SUPPORTED CHILD CARE CENTERS

Companies Most Frequently Cited	Location
Corning	Corning, NY
Fel-Pro	Skokie, IL
Hoffman LaRoche	Nutley, NJ
John Hancock	Boston, MA
Johnson & Johnson	New Brunswick, NJ
Johnson Wax	Racine, WI
Merck & Co.	Rahway, NJ
Patagonia	Ventura, CA
Stride Rite	Cambridge, MA

Additional Companies	Location
Allstate Insurance Co.	Charlotte, NC
America West Airlines	Phoenix, AZ
American Airlines, Inc.	Dallas, TX
American Bankers Insurance Group	Miami, FL
Amoco Corp.	Houston, TX

Additional Companies

Company	Location
Apple Computer	Cupertino, CA
Arlington County Public Schools	Arlington, VA
Barrett Bank	Jacksonville, FL
Baxter International	Deerfield, IL
BE&K Engineering and Construction	Birmingham, AL
Ben & Jerry's	Waterbury, VT
Berkshire Life	Pittsfield, MA
Blue Cross and Blue Shield	North Quincy, MA
Boston Public Schools	Boston, MA
Bowles Corp.	North Ferrisburg, VT
Business Office Supply Co.	Louisville, KY
Byrne Electrical Specialists, Inc.	Rockford, MI
Campbell Soup Co.	Camden, NJ
Centel Corp.	Chicago, IL
Champion International	Hamilton, Ohio & Stamford, CT
Chrysler	Huntsville, AL
Cigna	Philadelphia, PA
Citibank	New York, NY
CMP Publications, Inc.	Manhasset, NY
Colonial Williamsburg Foundation	Williamsburg, VA
Commerce Insurance Co.	Webster, MA
Dayton Hudson Corp.	Minneapolis, MN
Dominion Bankshares Corp.	Roanoke, VA
Dow Chemical Co.	Midland, MI
DuPont	Wilmington, DE
Fleetguard, Inc.	Lake Mills, IN
Frontier Cooperative Herbs	Norway, IN
Gannet:Courier-Journal	Louisville, KY
Genentech, Inc.	San Francisco, CA
General Motors	Flint, MI
Georgia Baptist Medical Center	Atlanta, GA
Glaxo, Inc.	Research Triangle Park, NC
Great Western Finance Corp.	Los Angeles, CA
Grieco Bros., Inc.	Lawrence, MA
Group 243, Inc.	Ann Arbor, MI
G.T. Water Products	Moorpark, CA
Haemonetics	Braintree, MA
HBO	Los Angeles, CA

Additional Companies	Location
Heart of the Valley Center	Corvallis, OR
Hershey Foods Corp.	Hershey, PA
Hewitt Assoc.	Lincolnshire, IL
Hill, Holiday, Connors, Cosmopulos, Inc.	Boston, MA
Honeywell	Minneapolis, MN
Household International	Prospect Heights, IL
Kingston Warren	Newfield, NH
Lancaster Laboratories	Lancaster, PA
Lego Systems, Inc.	Enfield, CT
Lincoln National Corp.	Green Bay, WI
Little Tykes Co.	Hudson, OH
Lomes Financial Group	Dallas, TX
Los Angeles Water & Power	Los Angeles, CA
Lotus Development Corp.	Cambridge, MA
Lucasarts Entertainment Co.	Skywalker Ranch, CA
McDonnell Douglas	St. Louis, MO
Marquette Electronics	Milwaukee, WI
Marriot Corp.	Washington, DC
Maui Land & Pineapple Co.	Kahului, HI
MBNA America Bank	Newark, DE
Mentor Graphics, Corp.	Wilsonville, OR
MONY	Syracuse, NY
Motorola	Libertyville, IL
National Medical Enterprises	Santa Monica, CA
Nations Bank	Charlotte, NC
Neuville Industries	Hildebran, NC
New London Trust	New London, NH
Nike	Beaverton, OR
Northern Trust Corp.	Chicago, IL
Nyloncraft	Mishawalca, IN
NYNEX	New York, NY
Official Airline Guides	Oak Brook, IL
Oliver Wright	Essex Junction, VT
Overseas Adventure Travel	Cambridge, MA
Pacific Presbyterian Medical Center	San Francisco, CA
Paramount Pictures Corp.	Los Angeles, CA
Phoenix Home Life	Enfield, CT

Additional Companies	Location
Proctor & Gamble	Cincinnati, OH
Prudential	Woodbridge, NJ
Quad/Graphics, Inc.	Pewaukee, WI
RAMCO	Fall River, MA
Rich's Department Store	Atlanta, GA
Riverside Methodist Hospital	Columbus, OH
St. Paul Fire & Marine Insurance Corp.	St. Paul, MN
St. Petersburg Times	St. Petersburg, FL
Samuel Goldwyn	Los Angeles, CA
Sara Lee	Chicago, IL
SAS Institute, Inc.	Cary, NC
Saturn Corp.	Troy, MI
Schering-Plough	Memphis, TN
Seattle Times	Seattle, WA
Shawnee Group	Shawnee-on-Delaware, PA
Syntex	Palo Alto, CA
Terry, Dunning & Terry	Mashpee, MA
Time Warner	New York, NY
Toyota	Georgetown, KY
Trammell Crow Co.	Dallas, TX
UNUM Life Insurance Co.	Portland, ME
U.S. Hosiery	Lincolnton, NC
USA Group	Fishers, IN
Visiting Nurses Association	Worchester, MA
Wang Laboratories, Inc.	Lowell, MA
Wear-Guard	Norwell, MA
Wegman's	Greece, NY
Williams & Watts, Inc.	West Caldwell, NJ
World Bank	Washington, DC
Zale Corp.	Dallas, TX

PARTIAL LISTING OF CONSORTIA CENTERS

Consortia	Location
Administrative Office of the United States Courts	Washington, DC
Architect of the Capitol	
Federal Judicial Center	

Consortia	Location
Judicial Panel on Multidistrict Litigation	Washington, DC
U.S. Sentencing Commission	
U.S. Supreme Court	
SMAL	
WDVM	
WJLA	
WRC	
WTTG	
Atlanta Journal Constitution	Atlanta, GA
Federal Reserve Bank of Atlanta	
First Atlanta	
Georgia Pacific Corporation	
Rich's Department Store	
Centers for Disease Control	Atlanta, GA
Emory University	
Henrietta Egleston Hospital for Children	
Beth Israel Hospital	Boston, MA
Brigham & Women's Hospital	
Children's Hospital	
Dana-Farber Cancer Institute	
Harvard Medical School	
Harvard School of Public Health	
Joslin Diabetes Center	
MASCO	
Simmons College	
The Winsor School	
Artificial Intelligence	Waltham, MA
Graphic Communications	
GTE Laboratories	
Henco Software	
Professional Council	
Prospect Hill Executive Office Park	
Sasaki Associates	

Consortia	Location
Babson College Wellesley College	Wellesley, MA

Coughlin Electrons, Inc.
Fletcher, Tilton & Whipple
Greenberg, Rosenblatt, Kull &
   Bitsoli
Lutheran House of Worcester
Paul Revere Insurance
Worcester County Institution
   for Savings
	Worcester, MA

Baltimore Gas and Electric C & P Telephone Company First National Bank of Maryland Maryland National Bank Mercantile Safe Deposit and Trust Company	Baltimore, MD
AIL System, Inc. Ariel Graphics General Instruments, Inc. Grumman Corporation IBM Long Island Savings Bank Nikon	Bethpage, NY

PARTIAL LISTING OF EMPLOYER-SUPPORTED HOSPITAL CENTERS

Hospitals	Location
Altoona Hospital	Altoona, PA
Anne Arundel Medical Center	Annapolis, MD
Arlington Hospital	Arlington, VA
Baptist Hospital of Miami	Miami, FL
Berkshire Medical Center	Pittsfield, MA
Beth Israel Hospital of Boston	Boston, MA
Boldgett Memorial Medical Center	Grand Rapids, MI

Hospitals	Location
Clifton Springs Hospital and Clinic	Clifton Springs, NY
Columbia Hospital for Women	Washington, DC
Emerson Hospital	Boston, MA
Fair Oaks Hospital	Fairfax, VA
Fairfax Hospital	Falls Church, VA
Georgia Baptist Medical Center	Atlanta, GA
Good Samaritan Hospital	Baltimore, MD
Hazelton Memorial Hospital	Hazelton, PA
Howard University Hospital	Washington, DC
Immanuel Memorial Hospital	Omaha, NE
Iowa Methodist Medical Center	Des Moines, IA
Jewish Hospital Healthcare Services	Louisville, KY
Lutheran General Hospital	Park Ridge, IL
Manchester Memorial Hospital	Manchester, CT
Monongalia General Hospital	Morgantown, WV
Mt. Vernon Hospital	Alexandria, VA
New England Medical Center Hospital	Boston, MA
Pacific Presbyterian Medical Center	San Francisco, CA
Prince George's Hospital	Cheverly, MD
Prince William Hospital	Manassas, VA
Riverside Methodist Hospital	Columbus, OH
St. Elizabeth Hospital	Appleton, WI
St. Francis Medical Center	Grand Island, NE
St. Mary's Health Center	St. Louis, MO
St. Vincent's Hospital	Birmingham, AL
Schumbert Medical Center	Shreveport, LA
Waltham-Weston Hospital	Waltham, MA
Winchester Hospital	Winchester, MA

PARTIAL LISTING OF EMPLOYER-SUPPORTED COLLEGE/ UNIVERSITY CENTERS

Colleges/Universities	Location
American University	Washington, DC
Amherst College	Amherst, MA

Colleges/Universities	Location
Arizona State University	Tempe, AZ
Bellevue Community College	Bellevue, WA
Boston University	Boston, MA
Brandeis University	Waltham, MA
Central Texas College	Killeen, TX
Cleveland State University	Cleveland, OH
Cornell University	Ithaca, NY
Duquesne University	Pittsburgh, PA
Gallaudet University	Washington, DC
George Mason University	Fairfax, VA
Georgetown Law School	Washington, DC
Georgia State University	Atlanta, GA
Harvard University	Cambridge, MA
Howard University	Washington, DC
Kansas State University	Manhattan, KS
Lafayette College	Easton, PA
Long Island University	Greenvale, NY
Massachusetts Institute of Technology	Cambridge, MA
Ohio State University	Columbus, OH
Pace University	New York, NY
Smith College	Northampton, MA
Southern Illinois University	Edwardsville, IL
Tufts University	Medford, MA
Tulane University	New Orleans, LA
University of Arkansas at Little Rock	Little Rock, AR
University of California	Oakland, CA
University of Maryland	College Park, MD
University of Massachusetts— Boston	Boston, MA
University of Minnesota at St. Paul Minneapolis	Minneapolis, MN
University of New Mexico	Albuquerque, NM
University of North Dakota	Grand Forks, ND
University of Pittsburgh	Pittsburgh, PA
University of South Florida	Tampa, FL
University of the District of Columbia	Washington, DC

Colleges/Universities	Location
University of Wisconsin—Stout	Menomonie, WI
Wheaton College	Norton, MA
William Rainey Harper College	Palatine, IL
Yale University	New Haven, CT

PARTIAL LISTING OF EMPLOYER-SUPPORTED FAMILY CHILD CARE NETWORKS

Companies	Location
America West Airlines	Phoenix, AZ
Baystate Medical Center	Springfield, MA
Donnely Corp.	Holland, MI
Eastman Kodak Co.	Rochester, NY
Hasbro, Inc.	Pawtucket, RI
Lincoln National	Fort Wayne, IN
Lost Arrow Corp.	Ventura, CA
New England Deaconess Associates	Concord, MA
Steelcase	Grand Rapids, MI

Appendix C

Child Care Center Liability Insurance Carriers

Note: Based on a list initially prepared by *Child Care Information Exchange.*

CIGNA Child Care Insurance Services
1600 Arch Street
Philadelphia, PA 19103
(800) 523-2710
(215) 523-3993

Frontier Insurance Company
Rhulen Insurance
217 Broadway
Monticello, NY 12701
(914) 794-8000
(800) 431-1270

General Star National Insurance Company
c/o Seabury & Smith
1166 Avenue of the Americas
New York, NY 10036
(800) 631-8890
Fax: (212) 345-4054

Lexington Insurance Company
National Insurance Professionals Corp.
2601 Fourth Avenue, Suite 200
Seattle, WA 98121

(800) ASK-NIPC (275-6472)
(206) 441-7960

Penn-America Insurance Company
420 S. York Road
Hatboro, PA 19040
(215) 443-3600

Reliable Insurance Company
THOMCO
P.O. Box 723035
Atlanta, GA 30339

Scottsdale Insurance Company
8877 North Gainey Center Drive
Scottsdale, AZ 85261
(800) 423-7675, ext. 3010
(602) 948-0505

U.S. Liability Insurance Company
Mt. Vernon Fire Insurance Company
U.S. Underwriters Insurance Company
1030 Continental Drive
King of Prussia, PA 19406
(215) 688-2535

Appendix
D

■ ■ ■ ■ ■

Current Child Day Care Licensing Offices

Note: Reprinted from "Current State Day Care Licensing Offices," *Child Care Action Campaign Information Guide 28* (New York: Child Care Action Campaign).

Alabama

Alabama Department of Human Resources
50 N. Ripley Street
Montgomery, AL 36130
(205) 261-5360

Alaska

Department of Health & Social Services
Division of Family and Youth Services
230 S. Franklin Street, Suite 206
Juneau, AK 99801
(907) 465-3013

Arizona

Arizona Department of Health Services
Office of Children, Day Care Facilities Division
100 W. Clarendon Street, 4th Floor
Phoenix, AZ 85013
(602) 255-1272

Arkansas

Division of Children & Family Services
Day Care Licensing Division
P.O. Box 1437
Little Rock, AR 72203
(501) 682-8590

California

Community Care Licensing
Department of Social Services, Day
   Care Unit
744 P Street, Mail Station 19-50
Sacramento, CA 95814
(916) 324-4031

Colorado

Department of Social Services
Day Care Unit
605 Bannock Street, Room 354
Denver, CO 80204
(303) 893-7166

Connecticut

Community Nursing Home
   Health Division
Child Day Care Licensing Unit
141-150 Washington Street
Hartford, CT 06106
(203) 566-2575

Delaware

Licensing Bureau
Delaware Youth and Family Center
1825 Faulkland Road
Wilmington, DE 19805-1195
(302) 633-2695

District of Columbia

Licensing & Certification
   Division
Social Services Branch
614 H Street, N.W.
Room 1031
Washington, DC 20001
(202) 727-7226

Florida

Office of Children, Youth &
   Families
Department of Health and
   Rehabilitative Services
1317 Winewood Boulevard
Tallahassee, FL 32399
(904) 488-4900

Georgia

Child Care Licensing Office
Department of Human Resources
878 Peachtree Street, N.E., Room
   607
Atlanta, GA 30309
(404) 894-5688

Guam

Division of Social Services
P.O. Box 2816
Agana, Guam 96910
011-671-734-7399

Hawaii

Department of Human Services
Licensing Unit
420 Weiaka Milo Road, Suite 101
Honolulu, HI 96817-4941
(808) 832-5025

Idaho

Department of Health & Welfare
Family and Children's Division
4355 Emerald Street, 2nd Floor
Boise, ID 83706
(208) 334-6800

Illinois

**Department of Children &
  Family Services**
406 E. Monroe Avenue
Springfield, IL 62701-1498
(217) 785-2598

Indiana

**State of Indiana, Department of
  Public Welfare**
Child Welfare/Social Service
  Division
402 W. Washington Street, Room
  W364
Indianapolis, IN 46204
(317) 232-4440

Iowa

**Division of Adult, Children &
  Family Services**
Iowa Department of Human
  Services
Hoover State Office Building
Des Moines, IA 50319
(515) 281-6074

Kansas

**Kansas Department of Health &
  Environment**
Landom State Office Building
Child Care License Section
900 S.W. Jackson Street
Topeka, KS 66612-1290
(913) 296-1275

Kentucky

**Division of Licensing and
  Regulation**
Cabinet for Human Resources
Building, 4th Floor East
Frankfort, KY 40621
(502) 564-2800

Louisiana

Department of Social Services
Department of Health & Hospitals
P.O. Box 3767/P.O. Box 3078
Baton Rouge, LA 70821
(504) 342-6446

Maine

Department of Human Services
Bureau of Child & Family Services
221 State Street
Augusta, ME 04333
(207) 289-5060

Maryland

**Office of Licensing and
  Certification**
Division of Child Care Centers
4201 Patterson Avenue
Baltimore, MD 21215
(301) 764-2750

Massachusetts

Office for Children
10 West Street
Boston, MA 02111
(617) 727-8956

Michigan

Division of Child Day Care Licensing
Michigan Department of Social Services
P.O. Box 30037, 235 S. Grand Street, Suite 1212
Lansing, MI 48909
(517) 373-8300

Minnesota

Department of Human Services
Division of Licensing
444 LaFayette Road
St. Paul, MN 55155-3842
(612) 296-3971

Mississippi

Division of Child Care & Special Licensure
Mississippi State Department of Health
P.O. Box 1700
Jackson, MS 39215-1700
(601) 960-7504

Missouri

State Department of Social Services
Division of Family Services
State Office of Child Care
Licensing Unit
P.O. Box 88
Jefferson City, MO 65103
(314) 751-2450

Montana

Department of Family Services
P.O. Box 8005
Helena, MT 59604
(406) 444-5900

Nebraska

Department of Social Services
P.O. Box 95026, 301 Centennial Mall South, 5th Floor
Lincoln, NE 68509-5062
(402) 471-3121

Nevada

Bureau of Services for Child Care
505 E. King Street, Room 101
Carson City, NV 89710
(702) 687-5911

New Hampshire

Division of Public Health Services
Bureau of Child Care Standards & Licensing
Health & Human Services Building
6 Hazen Drive
Concord, NH 03301
(603) 271-4624

New Jersey

Bureau of Licensing
Division of Youth & Family Services
CN 717
Trenton, NJ 08625-0717
(609) 292-9220

New Mexico

**Licensing Health-Related
  Facilities**
Public Health Division
1190 St. Francis Drive
Santa Fe, NM 87503
(505) 827-2389

New York

Bureau of Day Care Licensing
65 Worth Street, 4th Floor
New York, NY 10013
(212) 334-7803

**New York State Department of
  Social Services**
40 N. Pearl Street
Albany, NY 12243
(800) 342-3715

North Carolina

**Office of Child Day Care
  Licensing**
Child Day Care Section
701 Barbour Drive
Raleigh, NC 27603
(919) 733-4801

North Dakota

**North Dakota Department of
  Human Services**
Children & Family Services
  Division
Judicial Wing, 3rd Floor
600 E. Boulevard Avenue
Bismarck, ND 58505-0250
(701) 224-3580

Ohio

Office of Child Care Services
30 E. Broad Street, 30th Floor
Columbus, OH 43266-0423
(614) 466-3822

Oklahoma

Department of Human Services
Child Care Licensing Unit
P.O. Box 25352
Oklahoma City, OK 73125
(405) 521-3561

Oregon

Department of Human Services
Children's Services Division
198 Commercial Street, S.E.
Salem, OR 97310
(503) 378-3178

Pennsylvania

**Pennsylvania Department of
  Public Welfare**
Central Region Day Care Services
P.O. Box 2675, Lanco Lodge
  Building 25
Harrisburg, PA 17105
(717) 787-8691

Puerto Rico

Department of Social Services
Family Services Secretary
P.O. Box 11398, Fernandez Juncos
  Station
Santurce, Puerto Rico 00910
(809) 723-2127

Rhode Island

Department of Children & Their Families
Day Care Licensing Unit
610 Mount Pleasant Avenue, Building 2
Providence, RI 02908
(401) 457-4708

South Carolina

South Carolina Department of Social Services
Day Care Licensing Division
P.O. Box 1520
Columbia, SC 29202-1520
(803) 734-5740

South Dakota

Department of Social Services
Child Protection Services
Richard F. Kneip Building
700 Governor's Drive
Pierre, SD 57501-2291
(605) 773-3227

Tennessee

Day Care Licensing Division
Tennessee Department of Human Services
P.O. Box 1135, 1000 Second Avenue
Nashville, TN 37202
(615) 244-9706

Texas

Texas Department of Human Services
Day Care Licensing Division
P.O. Box 149030, W-403
Austin, TX 78714-9030
(512) 450-3261

Utah

Division of Human Services
Office of Licensing
120 North, 200 West
Salt Lake City, UT 84145
(801) 538-4242

Vermont

Licensing & Regulations Division
Day Care Unit
Department of Social & Rehabilitative Services
103 S. Main Street
Waterbury, VT 05676
(802) 241-2158

Virgin Islands

Department of Human Services
Barbel Plaza South
St. Thomas, Virgin Islands 00801
(809) 774-9030

Virginia

Division of Licensing Programs
Department of Social Services
Tyler Building, Suite 219
8007 Discovery Drive
Richmond, VA 23239
(804) 662-9025

Washington

Department of Social & Health Services
Division of Children & Family Services
P.O. Box 45710
Olympia, WA 98504
(206) 586-2688

West Virginia

West Virginia Department of Human Resources
Office of Social Services
Building 6, Room 850
Charleston, WV 25305
(304) 348-7980

Wisconsin

Day Care Licensing
Department of Health and Social Services
3601 Memorial Drive
Madison, WI 53704
(608) 249-0441

Wyoming

Division of Public Assistance & Social Services
Family Services Unit
Hathaway Building, 3rd Floor
Cheyenne, WY 82002
(307) 777-7561

Appendix
E

▨ ▨ ▨ ▨ ▨

Resources for Playground
Information

Baker, Katherine R. *Let's Play Outdoors*. Washington, DC: National Association for the Education of Young Children, 1991.

Frost, Joe L. *Play and Playscapes*. Albany, NY: Delmar Publications, 1992.

Frost, Joe L., and Sue C. Wortham. "Evolution of American Playgrounds." *Young Children* 43 (July 1988).

Jambor, Tom, and Richard Gargiulo. "The Playground: A Social Entity for Mainstreaming." *JOPERD* (October 1987).

Morrison, Melanie. "A Human Factors Approach to Design" (paper, Children First, January 1993).

Morrison, Melanie, and Mary Ellen Fise. *Report & Model Law on Public Play Equipment and Areas*. Washington, DC: Consumer Federation of America, 1992.

National Association for the Education of Young Children. *Healthy Young Children*. Washington, DC: National Association for the Education of Young Children, 1991.

Olds, Anita, and George Kousoulas. *Architectural Prototype Documents*. Study for the Development of Day Care Centers in State Facilities, Commonwealth of Massachusetts. (January 1987).

U.S. Consumer Product Safety Commission. *Handbook for Playground Safety*. Washington, DC: U.S. Consumer Product Safety Commission, 1991.

Appendix
F

A Sampling of Architectural Firms with Child Care Center Experience

Einhorn, Yaffee & Prescott
Argus Building
Broadway at Beaver Street
Albany, NY 12207

Ellerbe Becket
1875 Connecticut Avenue, N.W.,
   Suite 600
Washington, DC 20009

Garcia/Myodo
2219 Roosevelt
Berkeley, CA 94703

Mullins, Freeman & White
1691 Phoenix Boulevard, Suite 270
Atlanta, GA 30349

Rothman, Rothman, Heineman
711 Atlantic Avenue
Boston, MA 02111

RTKL Associates
400 E. Pratt Street
Baltimore, MD 21202

**Smith, Hynchman & Grylls
   Associates**
150 W. Jefferson Avenue, Suite 100
Detroit, MI 48226

Tippett, Clepper & Associates
3715 Northside Parkway, N.E.
Building 200, Suite 650
Atlanta, GA 30327

Weihe Partnership
1666 K Street, N.W.
Washington, DC 20006

Whitneybell Architects, Inc.
1102 Missouri Avenue
Phoenix, AZ 85014-2784

Appendix G

Resource Organizations

ACCCI: Society for Work Family Professionals
P.O. Box 77345
Atlanta, GA 30357
(615) 251-1160

Child Care Action Campaign (CCAC)
330 Seventh Avenue, 17th Floor
New York, NY 10001
(212) 239-0138

Child Care Information Exchange
P.O. Box 2890
Redmond, WA 98073
(206) 883-9394

Child Care Law Center
22 Second Street
San Francisco, CA 94105
(415) 495-5498

National Association for the Education of Young Children (NAEYC)
1509 16th Street, N.W.
Washington, DC 20036-1426
(800) 424-2460 or
(202) 232-8777

The National Work Family Alliance
52 Chestnut Street
Boston, MA 02108
(617) 248-0809

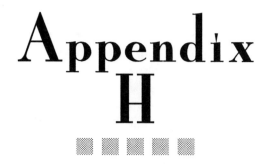

Appendix H

Child Care Program Inventory (CCPI)
Evaluation Criteria

I. STAFF-CHILD INTERACTIONS

GOAL: To ensure that staff/child interactions be characterized by warmth, respect, and responsiveness.

This is achieved when

- Teachers focus on *individual children* more than the whole group.
- Interactions encourage child involvement and exploration with materials and peers.
- Teachers use open-ended questions to encourage children to describe their feelings and experiences.
- Teachers guide children's behavior with positive techniques such as redirection, positive reinforcement, and planning.

INVENTORY ITEMS:

(Based on observing the program and interviewing teachers)

	RATING		
	Occasionally	*Most of the time*	*Almost always*
1) Staff interact nonverbally by frequent smiling, touching, and holding.	1	2	3
2) Staff talk with *individual children* throughout daily routines (arriving, departing, eating, diapering) and activities	1	2	3
3) Staff respond to *individual children's* questions and requests	1	2	3
4) Staff listen to *individual children* with respect.	1	2	3
5) Staff encourage children to use language to describe their feelings to solve problems ...	1	2	3
6) Staff ask children open-ended questions	1	2	3
7) Staff help *individual children* get involved in activities	1	2	3
8) Staff use positive approaches to help children behave constructively	1	2	3
9) Children are under adult supervision at all times	1	2	3

COMMENTS:

_____

_____

_____

_____

_____

_____

II. CURRICULUM

GOAL: To ensure that the curriculum provides opportunities for children to learn through active involvement with developmentally appropriate materials and experiences.

This is achieved when

- Play is encouraged and respected.
- Experiences and activities are **concrete and experiential**.
- Teachers function as facilitators—not directors—of children's play by **responding** to and extending their interests and ideas.
- Materials and equipment reflect the *diversity* that exists in the Center and in our society.
- There is a balance of activities throughout the day (indoor/outdoor, quiet/active, individual/small group/large group, large muscle/small muscle, child initiated/adult initiated).
- Staff provide opportunities for children to *choose from several activities*.
- The environment is *child centered*.

INVENTORY ITEMS:

(Based on observing the program and interviewing teachers)

	RATING		
	Occasionally	*Most of the time*	*Almost always*
1) Throughout each day there is an opportunity for children to be involved in			
-indoor and outdoor activities	1	2	3
-quiet and active activities	1	2	3
-individual, small group, and large group activities	1	2	3
-large muscle and small muscle activities ...	1	2	3
-child-initiated and adult-initiated activities	1	2	3
2) There are a variety and sufficient quantity of developmentally appropriate **hands-on** materials:			
-active play equipment	1	2	3
-building materials	1	2	3
-puzzles, manipulative toys	1	2	3
-books, musical instruments	1	2	3
-art materials	1	2	3
-dramatic play props	1	2	3
-sensory materials (such as sand and water)	1	2	3

	RATING		
	Occasionally	*Most of the time*	*Almost always*
3) Children are exposed to the diversity in our society (such as variety in clothing, food, music, hairstyle, skin color) throughout their day, through planned and spontaneous activities and materials:			
-books	1	2	3
-music	1	2	3
-cooking activities	1	2	3
-dramatic play props	1	2	3
-art materials	1	2	3
4) Children choose from among several available activities	1	2	3
5) Teachers respect children's right not to participate in some activities	1	2	3
6) Teachers encourage children to explore freely with materials	1	2	3
7) Teachers encourage children to focus on the process of doing and making not on the product itself. (e.g., **building** with blocks, **cutting, painting, drawing, gluing, pasting**)	1	2	3
8) Teachers involve children in play by -**extending** their ideas and interest	1	2	3
-**responding** to their cues (verbal and nonverbal)	1	2	3
9) Children's own work is displayed attractively around the Center, reflecting the process of their activity rather than the product of teacher-designed projects	1	2	3

COMMENTS:

_____

_____

_____

_____

_____

_____

III. STAFF-PARENT INTERACTIONS

GOAL: To ensure that parents are an integral part of the Center's program.

This is achieved when

- Parents are welcome to visit and participate in the Center program.
- There are *formal mechanisms* for parent-staff communication, such as a Parent Handbook, Center Newsletter, parent orientation process, parent-teacher conferences.
- There are *informal mechanisms* for parent-staff communication, such as opportunities for "chats" about home and Center approaches toward child-rearing, and parent participation in Center activities such as field trips.

INVENTORY ITEMS:

(Based on observing the program and interviewing teachers)

	RATING		
	Occasionally	Most of the time	Almost always
1) New parents are **formally** oriented to the Center through			
-Center tour	1	2	3
-Parent Handbook with Center's philosophy, procedures, and policies	1	2	3
2) Parents receive a periodic Center Newsletter	1	2	3
3) There are regular parent-teacher conferences	1	2	3
4) Parents have regular opportunities to talk informally with their child's primary caregiver	1	2	3
5) Parents participate in field trips, birthday parties and other Center events	1	2	3

COMMENTS:

_____

_____

_____

_____

_____

_____

IV. STAFFING

GOAL: To ensure that the Center's program is staffed by adults who understand child development and early childhood educational practices and that the Center's staffing patterns meet the social, emotional, physical, and cognitive needs of the children.

This is achieved when

- Teachers have formal training in early childhood education/child development.
- New staff are oriented about Center philosophy, policies, and procedures.
- The Center provides regular training opportunities to enable teachers to develop professionally, and to meet the changing needs of children and parents.
- The *number* of children in a group is limited to facilitate adult-child interaction.
- The child-staff *ratios* within each group are sufficient to facilitate adult-child interaction.
- Each staff member has primary responsibility for an identified group of children to ensure **continuity of care**.

INVENTORY ITEMS:

(Based on interviewing the director and/or the teachers)

	RATING		
	Occasionally	*Most of the time*	*Almost always*
1) New staff are **formally** oriented to the Center about			
-program philosophy and procedures	1	2	3
-guidance and classroom management techniques	1	2	3
-emergency health and safety procedures ...	1	2	3
2) Ongoing staff training addresses the following areas:			
-health and safety	1	2	3
-child development	1	2	3
-guidance and discipline techniques	1	2	3
-curriculum	1	2	3
-communication skills	1	2	3

COMMENTS:

_____

_____

_____

_____

V.   ADMINISTRATION

GOAL: To ensure that Center policies and practices reflect the needs and interests of children, parents and staff, and that the Center is in compliance with state and local regulations.

This is achieved when

- There is long-range fiscal planning.
- Written personnel policies detail job descriptions, performance evaluations, staff benefits, compensation, resignation and termination, and grievance procedures.
- There are written operating policies and procedures.
- There are systematic mechanisms for staff communication.
- The role of the board of directors is clearly defined.

INVENTORY ITEMS:

(Based on reviewing written policies and documents, and interviewing the director and the teachers)

INVENTORY ITEMS	RATING	
	YES	*NO*
1) Administrative policies and procedures are clearly written for		
-Center operations, including hours, holidays, fees, and illness		
-personnel, including job descriptions, compensations, resignation and termination, benefits, and grievance procedures		
-reporting suspected cases of child abuse or neglect		
-dealing with emergency situations, such as medical emergencies or building evacuation		
-preparing and/or serving food in compliance with legal requirements for nutrition and food service........................		
-a governing Board of Directors, defining roles and responsibilities of board members and staff...........................		
2) Fiscal records are kept with evidence of long-range budgeting and sound financial planning		

	RATING	
	YES	*NO*

3) Program administrators and staff meet regularly to discuss

-program plans, including curriculum and Center procedures ....

-the needs of individual children and families ....

-staff development needs ....

4) Staff members are provided space and time away from children each day ....

5) Staff are provided paid planning time ....

6) The Center is in compliance with the legal requirements for protection of the health and safety of children in group settings ......

7) The last safety inspection of the physical plant was conducted on_____

8) Please indicate the number of children currently receiving tuition subsidies or scholarships. _____

9) What was the dollar amount budgeted for tuition subsidies in the last fiscal year? _____

10) What was the actual amount used for tuition subsidies in the last fiscal year?

ATTACHMENTS:

Please attach copies of the following documents:

_____1) State license

_____2) Recent financial audit

_____3) Board/vendor contract or agreement

COMMENTS:

_____

_____

_____

_____

_____

_____

VI. CENTER ENVIRONMENT

GOAL: To ensure that the Center's physical environment is *safe, comfortable, and conducive to children's growth and development.*
  This is achieved when

- The indoor and outdoor environments are safe, clean, attractive, spacious, and appropriately equipped.

- Indoor space is arranged to accommodate the variety of **activities** appropriate for **individuals, small groups, and large groups** of children of different *developmental levels.* (For example: carpeted areas and crawling space for infants and toddlers; clearly defined play areas so that children can work individually, in small groups, or in large groups in *all developmental domains* [dramatic play, construction, **manipulatives, open-ended art, music, and quiet reading**]).

INVENTORY ITEMS:

(Based on observations)

	RATING	
	YES	*NO*
1) Indoor space includes the following elements:		
-safe, well-maintained equipment		
-well-lighted and ventilated rooms		
-sound-absorbing materials to minimize excessive noise		
-soft elements such as rugs, cushions, or rocking chairs		
-storage space for children's and adults' personal belongings		
2) Outdoor space includes cushioning materials such as mats, wood chips, or sand under equipment		
3) INFANT space has carpeted areas, crawling space, and sturdy furniture so nonwalkers can pull themselves up or balance themselves while walking		
4) TODDLER and PRESCHOOL activity areas are organized with clear pathways for children to move from one area to another with minimal distractions		

	RATING	
	YES	*NO*

5) Activities are clustered together into areas, such as block play, dramatic play, open-ended art, woodwork, and water play ....

6) There are private areas for children to look at books or to play by themselves while being supervised ....

7) Hazardous materials such as cleaning products and medicines are kept in a locked area away from children ....

COMMENTS:

_____

_____

_____

_____

_____

_____

Note: This form was developed by Fried & Sher, Inc., based on the accreditation criteria of the National Academy of Early Childhood Programs of NAEYC.

Appendix
I

Application for Board of Directors

Date _____

Your answers to the following questions will help the board become more familiar with candidates for the board of directors.

1. Name _____

2. Job Title _____

3. Work Mailing
   Address _____

   _____

4. Please describe any experience you have had serving on a board for a nonprofit agency.

   _____

   _____

   _____

   _____

   _____

5. Please describe any experience you have had in early childhood education or a related field.

    _____

    _____

    _____

    _____

    _____

6. Please indicate whether you have interest in serving the center in any of the following areas:

    ■ Tuition assistance _____

    _____

    ■ Marketing _____

    _____

    ■ Special projects (please specify) _____

    _____

    ■ Fund-raising _____

    _____

7. Please add any additional information you would like us to have.

    _____

    _____

    _____

    _____

    _____

    _____

    _____

    _____

    _____

    _____

Index

by Janet Perlman